T0318957

Cambridge Elements ≡

Elements in Environmental Humanities
edited by
Louise Westling
University of Oregon
Timo Maran
University of Tartu
Serenella Iovino
University of North Carolina at Chapel Hill

FORCES OF REPRODUCTION

Notes for a Counter-Hegemonic Anthropocene

Stefania Barca
Centre for Social Studies, University of Coimbra

CAMBRIDGE
UNIVERSITY PRESS

CAMBRIDGE
UNIVERSITY PRESS

University Printing House, Cambridge CB2 8BS, United Kingdom

One Liberty Plaza, 20th Floor, New York, NY 10006, USA

477 Williamstown Road, Port Melbourne, VIC 3207, Australia

314–321, 3rd Floor, Plot 3, Splendor Forum, Jasola District Centre,
New Delhi – 110025, India

79 Anson Road, #06–04/06, Singapore 079906

Cambridge University Press is part of the University of Cambridge.

It furthers the University's mission by disseminating knowledge in the pursuit of
education, learning, and research at the highest international levels of excellence.

www.cambridge.org
Information on this title: www.cambridge.org/9781108813952
DOI: 10.1017/9781108878371

First published 2020

A catalogue record for this publication is available from the British Library.

ISBN 978-1-108-81395-2 Paperback
ISSN 2632-3125 (online)
ISSN 2632-3117 (print)

Forces of Reproduction

Notes for a Counter-Hegemonic Anthropocene

Elements in Environmental Humanities

DOI: 10.1017/9781108878371
First published online: November 2020

Stefania Barca
Centre for Social Studies, University of Coimbra
Author for correspondence: Stefania Barca, sbarca68@gmail.com

Abstract: The concept of Anthropocene has been incorporated within a hegemonic narrative that represents 'Man' as the dominant geological force of our epoch, emphasizing the destruction and salvation power of industrial technologies. This Element develops a counter-hegemonic narrative based on the perspective of earthcare labour– or the 'forces of reproduction'. It brings to the fore the historical agency of reproductive and subsistence workers as those subjects that, through both daily practices and organized political action, take care of the biophysical conditions for human reproduction, thus keeping the world alive. Adopting a narrative justice approach, and placing feminist political ecology right at the core of its critique of the Anthropocene storyline, this Element offers a novel and timely contribution to the Environmental Humanities.

Keywords: modern economic growth,decoloniality,eco/transfeminism, commoning,inter-species being

ISBNs: 9781108813952 (PB), 9781108878371 (OC)
ISSNs: 2632-3125 (online), 2632-3117 (print)

Contents

Would feminist authority and the power to name give the world a new identity, a new story?

(Haraway, 1991: 72)

The master's tools will never dismantle the master's house.

(Lorde, 1984)

Introduction

In May 2011, Zé Claudio Ribeiro da Silva and Maria do Espirito Santo, nut collectors and members of the agroforestry project (Projeto Agro-Extractivista, PAE) of Praialta Piranheira in the Brazilian Amazon, were brutally murdered as a consequence of their engagement in protecting the forest from illegal logging and timber trafficking (Milanez, 2015). Making a living from a non-exploitative and regenerative relationship with the forest, and passionate about the defence of the rights of both Amazonia and its people, Maria and Zé Claudio's deaths are among the number of earth defenders whose lives are being taken, year after year, for opposing the infinite expansion of global economic growth (Global Witness, 2017; Martínez-Alier, 2002). But their lives and labour belong to an even wider class, which Ariel Salleh (2010) has called the global meta-industrial labour class, made up of those less-than-humanized (racialized, feminized, dispossessed) subjects who reproduce humanity by taking care of the biophysical environment that makes life itself possible. I call them the forces of reproduction: they keep the world alive, yet their environmental agency goes largely unrecognized in mainstream narratives of that epoch of catastrophic earth-system changes that scientists have called the Anthropocene.

Narratives do not kill by themselves, of course. But they might hide the killings and the killed from view, and convince us that they are not part of the story of modernity; that this story is benign and a great achievement of human-ity, were it not for the limits that nature puts on human wealth and accomplish-ment. This, I argue, is the hegemonic narrative of the Anthropocene – and its hero is capitalist/industrial modernity. By this expression I mean a specific type of modernity – that which considers the forces of production (Western science and industrial technology) as the key driver of human progress and well-being. Emerging with the rise of capitalism, this narrative has been subsequently assumed as a universal model and maintained by State socialist regimes in different geo-historical contexts. This Element is devoted to displacing the hegemony of this narrative and allowing counter-hegemonic visions of mod-ernity to emerge.

I came to know about Zé Claudio and Maria from Felipe Milanez, a Brazilian reporter who had visited Praialta Piranheira while working on a documentary film about deforestation in the Amazon region only a few months before they were killed. He interviewed Zé Claudio and Maria about their life and work, and about the death threats they had been receiving for some time related to their engagement as forest defenders. I met Felipe a year later. He had been greatly affected by Zé Claudio and Maria's death, and was seeking ways to make sense of their story – so he decided to enrol in a PhD programme in Political Ecology at the University of Coimbra in Portugal, and we started to work together on different projects dedicated to making their story heard. This Element is born out of that long-term engagement. It asks the question: Why are the forces of reproduction not accounted for in the hegemonic Anthropocene narrative? Do they *count for nothing*[1] in the historical balance sheet of human/earth relationships?

This is, unequivocally, a feminist question – in fact, I would argue, this is the kind of feminist question that we need to ask if we want to *change the system, not the climate*. But it requires more than feminist answers. Questioning the at once exclusionary and normative character of the Anthropocene narrative, while making visible the alternate humanities that inhabit it, requires us to adopt an expanded version of feminism, one capable of weaving together ecological, decolonial, class and species perspectives. The Anthropocene would thus appear as an idea moulded by the privileged eye of the white/male subject of history – one which inevitably hides all those who are non-privileged, dehumanizing and making invisible those 'others' that actively oppose the systematic killing of nature. Inspired by the 'Black, lesbian, mother, warrior, poet' Audre Lorde (1984), I argue that the Anthropocene is nothing other than a master's house: one that imprisons both human and non-human nature in order to make them work for capital. Dismantling this master's house to liberate humanity and the earth requires formidable new tools, both material and symbolic.

Undoing the Anthropocene narrative is very relevant to, and indeed constitutive of, narrative justice, the project of telling the other-than-master stories of human habitation of the earth. We need narrative justice to make us see the killed. Their existence disturbs and disrupts the progressive narrative: if poor people put their lives before the advancement of progress into the Amazon forest, then something must be wrong with progress itself. My understanding of narrative justice is consistent with the invitation, coming from other scholars in the environmental humanities, to think of the Anthropocene concept with 'the obscene' (Swyngedouw and Ernstson, 2018), that is, those subjects who are

---

[1] I am deliberately paraphrasing the title of Marilyn Waring's book *Counting for nothing* (1987), a landmark contribution to ecofeminist and degrowth thought.

removed from the official representation, and that carry the possibility of re-politicizing it via both struggle and alternative life practices (Armiero and De Angelis, 2017).

I have been particularly inspired by Donna Houston's (2013) invitation to mobilize environmental justice storytelling as a method that connects 'biographical, political, philosophical and place-based meanings', forging a tool by which 'alternate knowledge' might be sustained and 'different futures might be enacted' (Houston, 2013: 419). I believe this responds to what Serpil Opperman and Serenella Iovino have described as a key task for the environmental humanities, that of calling for 'new modes of knowing and being' which might 'enable environmentally just practices' (Oppermann and Iovino, 2016: 2). In their view, this requires new narrative tools, allowing for 'stronger, more-than-human coalitions' (Opperman and Iovino, 2016: 19). This, I argue, needs to be done by attacking the core of the Anthropocene narrative: its politico-economic logic, what I term *eco-capitalist realism*. Hence this Element's critique of not only political economy but of historical materialism itself, with its classical emphasis on the forces of production. Making the forces of reproduction visible and accounted for, I argue, is a crucial task for environmental humanities scholarship, one that might help us develop a significantly new understanding of our epochal challenges and of the forces that can be mobilized to address them. Responding to such an urge for ecological revolution, this Element aims at telling the right story of climate and earth-system change, one where Zé Claudio and Maria are seen and their lives count.

Great inspiration comes, in this endeavour, from a landmark contribution of ecofeminist scholarship: Val Plumwood's *Feminism and the mastery of nature* (1993). Building upon two decades of ecofeminist critiques of hierarchical dualisms (Salleh, 2017[1997] ; Merchant, 1996), Plumwood argued that the problem at the root of the current ecological crisis was what she called the 'master model' of Western modernity. In Western thought, she explained, concepts of the human have been developed in similarity with those defining male identity; the problem, however, is neither the male sex as such nor the condition of being human, but the way in which Western culture has defined human identity vis-à-vis gender *and* nature. She described dualism as a hierarchical system of signification, which polarizes existing differences positing them as naturally given and irreconcilable separations – man/woman, mind/body, civilized/savage, human/nature – which 'correspond directly to and naturalise gender, class, race and nature oppressions respectively' (Plumwood, 1993: 43). One side is taken as naturally dominant and primary, while the other is defined in relation to it – in terms of lacking those qualities. Domination of one side over the other is thus seen as inherent in the order of things. In dualism, Plumwood explained, power forms identity by distorting both sides of what is split apart. Consequently, the proper response to dualism is neither reversal nor merger, annihilation of difference, but challenging the polarization of identities and reconstructing difference along non-hierarchical lines.

For example, rejecting the human/nature dualism does not mean reversing the relationship into one of the total submission of humanity to nature: 'We do not have to accept a choice between treating "nature" as our slave or treating it as our master' (Plumwood, 1993: 37), Plumwood wrote. Similarly, the reconstruction of women's difference must come to terms with 'the combined identity in which colonised and coloniser identities are interwoven' (Plumwood, 1993: 67): as Western women are not only colonized in relation to gender, but are themselves colonizers in relation to other racial, cultural, class and/or species identities, critical reconstruction of women's identity must involve a critique of the master model of the human. This is why, Plumwood claimed, the ecofeminist programme is a highly 'integrative' one, in the sense that it brings together cultural, socialist, Black and anti-colonial feminisms in challenging the structure of interrelated dualisms that correspond to several forms of repression, alienation and domination.

Although written in the early 1990s, *Feminism and the mastery of nature* still offers indispensable tools with which to analyse the planetary ecological crisis. It allows us to see how Western modernity identifies humanity with the male master of 'nature' – identifying women and racialized subjects with the latter. This identification, I argue, is reinstated by the hegemonic concept of Anthropocene, which assumes the master model of modernity as representing the entire human species, and denying the existence or historical relevance of non-master agencies and possibilities. Most importantly, then, Plumwood's critique of master modernity allows us to search for the alternate stories that are inscribed, largely invisible and untold, in the current epoch of human habitation of the earth. As she wrote:

> The power to direct, cast and script this ruling drama has been in the hands of only a tiny minority of the human race and of human cultures. Much inspiration for new, less destructive guiding stories can be drawn from sources other than the master, from subordinated and ignored parts of western culture, such as women's stories of care. (Plumwood, 1993: 196)

Uncovering these alternate stories, she concluded, is an important way of making visible and contributing to fostering those alternative rationalities which have contrasted with or simply survived the master model, with a view to 'realign reason' away from dualism and elite control and towards 'social formations built on radical democracy, co-operation and mutuality' (Plumwood, 1993: 196).

Building upon Plumwood's work, and on materialist ecofeminist thought more generally, this Element will show how the official Anthropocene narrative incorporates the master model of humanity with its built-in sex/gender, racial/colonial, class and species relations. Its key character, *the Anthropos, is an abstraction based on a white, male and heterosexual historical subject in possession of reason (qua science, technology and the law) and the means of production, by which tools it is entitled to extract labour and value from what it defines as Other.* This is, in fact, its civilizational mission – what legitimizes all its actions, including the worst atrocities. Contrary, however, to the official Anthropocene discourse, *this master humanity is not a species, that is, a natural, ahistorical subject, but a power system made up of material and symbolic relations.* Moreover, it has taken different configurations over time and place, in response to the resistance it has encountered from the Other. This is why its aim is totalizing: devouring the Other – both human and non-human – so that no resistance is opposed to its rule.

The Anthropocene narrative, I argue, is to be rejected: this is because by accepting it, we subscribe to the idea that history has come to an end and no more resistance is to be expected. That the world *is* what the master has made of it. That the Others are not historical subjects with a revolutionary potential, that they do not have any force, any power to oppose the master, because they are in fact organs of its universal body which obey its universal mind. If we accept that all humanity is one with the master, from where, then, should we expect change to come? The Anthropocene ideal wants us to believe that the master itself holds the capacity to address the ecological crisis. It claims that non-human nature – or a particular version of it represented by geology and climate – is now exercising historical agency by opposing its force to that of the master; and that the master will either respond to that force by changing its relationship with its environment or perish. That ideal is flawed – we should not put our hopes in it. For decades, the master has known that it is in serious danger, but it has not been capable of any effective response. It is simply proceeding along the only path it knows, defending itself with increasing ferocity against those who resist it. Our only hopes are with the resistance.

My counter-master narrative of the Anthropocene is based on the hypothesis that history consists in a struggle of other-than-master subjects for producing life, in its autonomy from capital and freedom of expression, a struggle that opposes the unlimited expansion of the master's rule. These other-than-master subjects are the *forces of reproduction*. In a rather asystematic way, the concept reflects the influence of, and attempts to merge, two distinct theoretical traditions: ecofeminist thought and historical materialism. Their critical intersection (Salleh 2017[1997]) allows us to see that the key commonality between all non-master Others is a broadly defined but still cogent notion of *labour*: from different positions, and in different forms, women, slaves, proletarians, animals and non-human nature are all made to work for the master. They must provide it with the necessities of life, so that it can devote itself to higher occupations. The master depends on them for its survival and wealth, but this dependency is constantly denied and the forces of reproduction are represented as lingering in the background of historical agency.

In Western thought, however, the concept of labour is deeply gendered: as Plumwood (1993: 25) recalled, human identity has been associated with concepts of productive labour, sociability and culture – thus, we can argue, it has been separated from supposedly lower forms of work (qua reproduction and care) and property relations (qua commoning). Capitalist political economy defines reproductive work as non-labour, that is, a valueless activity, although socially necessary to sustain the master; the commons is defined as waste – forms of not-yet-realized value, to be appropriated and improved upon by the master. True wealth and human emancipation can only come from the master's house, and from there trickle down to the rest. A new and supposedly higher form of production, premised on colonial/racial, gender, class and species inequalities, sits at the core of capitalist modernity, defining it with respect to non-capitalist modes of production, and has been rapidly universalized as a hegemonic model.

Merging historical materialism with ecofeminism leads us to look at the Anthropocene from the perspective of reproductive labour – the work of sustaining life in its material and immaterial needs. Subsistence farming, fishing and gathering, domestic work, gardening, teaching, nursing, healthcare, waste collecting and recycling are all forms of reproductive labour insofar as they are essential to the development of human nature in its interdependency with the non-human world. *By its own logic, reproductive labour opposes abstract social labour and all that objectifies and instrumentalizes life towards other ends.* Life itself is the product of (human and non-human) reproductive labour. At the same time, capitalism subjects this labour to increasing commodification and object-ification: this generates a contradiction insofar as reproductive labour becomes directly or indirectly incorporated within the money–commodity–money circuit of value. Capitalism thus diminishes or annihilates the life-enhancing potenti-alities of the forces of reproduction, turning them into instruments for accumu-lation. This process depletes both the worker and the environment, by extracting from them more work and energy than necessary and leaving them exhausted.

As Tithi Batthacharya (2019) has put it: 'Life-making increasingly conflicts with the imperatives of profit-making'.

Finally, my forces of reproduction are a queer political subject, in the sense that they point to both inter- and intra-species becoming; they describe not only material agency in daily subsistence practices (what is typically under-stood as 'women's work'), but also the potential, inherent in such agency, for rejecting heteropatriarchy and the sexual division of labour which are founda-tional to the master model of industrial modernity. Only by starting from this rejection, I argue, can reproductive and earthcare labour be seen and valued as tools for halting and reversing the ecological crisis. In this sense, my forces of reproduction describe a political subject in the making; they refer to the convergence (both ongoing and potential) of (trans)feminist, Indigenous, peasant, commoning, environmental justice, and other life-making struggles across the world, based on an emerging awareness that keeping the world alive requires dismantling the master's house. With their commitment to defending a life project of more-than-human commoning, Zé Claudio and Maria were part of this very struggle; their story survived their killing and became a seed of justice for those who continue to fight. This Element is intended to help spread that seed, in the hope that it will grow into global ecological class consciousness.

A Master's Narrative

At the opening plenary of the 2012 Rio+20 Earth Summit, delegates from all over the world were seated for the projection of a video called *Welcome to the Anthropocene*. Presented as 'A 3-minute journey through the last 250 years from the start of the Industrial revolution to today', the documentary was meant to offer a science-based, consensual understanding by which to make sense of the current earth-systems crisis and to frame the political choices to be made at the summit.[2] The video is now included in what is defined as 'the world's first educational web portal on the Anthropocene'. Promoted by several research centres, think-tanks and funding agencies in climate change and sustainability,[3] its declared aim is 'to inspire, educate and engage people about the interactions between humans and the planet'.

Although the Anthropocene is a highly contested concept in the social sciences and humanities, and different narratives exist regarding the historical roots of the ecological and climate crises, the particular version promoted in the video referred to above can be considered as the official Anthropocene

---

[2] See www.youtube.com/watch?v=pTk11idmTUA   [3] See www.anthropocene.info

storyline. Not only does it reflect 'the dominant climate discourse in the mainstream scientific and media arena' (Bonneuil and Fressoz, 2017), but – more importantly – it has been adopted by the United Nations Environment Programme (UNEP), thus becoming 'the hegemonic common sense' (Goodman and Salleh, 2013) concerning the climate and earth-system crisis. Since the first Earth Summit in Rio de Janeiro in 1992, this 'common sense' has orientated environmental decisions with life-and-death consequences upon the majority world – which is actually excluded from scientific and governance conversations. Holding the combined advantage of simplification and reflection of neoliberal power structures, this hegemonic Anthropocene common sense can be considered a master's narrative; thus undoing it requires an unprecedented effort at counter-mastering.

The video features an unspecified *We* subject who, having improved the lives of billions of humans, has become a phenomenal global force of earth-system change, threatening the continuation of life on earth. Enter the Anthropocene, *the most recent chapter of our history*. The story is depicted as starting in one particular place and moment – England 250 years ago – that is, coinciding with the spatio-temporality of what economic historians have termed the industrial revolution. For a certain time, the narrative goes, this was a success story of brilliant inventions sustained by fossil fuels, a success that spread from Europe to the rest of the world via global transportation networks that connected people from one side of the world to the other. Medical discoveries and chemical fertilizers accompanied this global success story, allowing for a sevenfold population increase in just one century. This tale of fossil-fuelled progress is shown to have witnessed a 'great acceleration' in the 1950s, when abrupt change came about: *globalization, marketing, tourism and huge investments* led to enormous economic growth, and massive urbanization turned cities into *even more powerful creative engines*. That point in human history is said to have improved *beyond measure* the lives of billions in terms of health, wealth, longevity and security: *never have so many had so much*, the narrating voice proclaims.

In the space of one generation, *We* is said to have reached the peak of its accomplishment, manifesting all its geological power: it now moves more rocks and sediments than all natural processes together and manages three-quarters of the earth's land surface. Here, the celebration becomes a gloomy account. It turns out that *We* is also emitting the highest levels of greenhouse gases in a million years, and is responsible for a hole in the ozone layer, the loss of biodiversity, the degradation of water systems, sea-level rises, ocean acidification and the near collapse of many earth-systems. All this testifies to the fact that *We* has entered a new geological epoch, one in which humanity is reshaping the earth. No need to despair, however: humanity is a force capable of great *creativity, energy and industry*. It has shaped the past, it is shaping the present, it can shape the future. *You and I* – the narrating voice concludes – are part of this story: we are the first generation to have realized our responsibility, that of finding *a safe operating space* within planetary boundaries, for the sake of future generations. *Welcome to the Anthropocene!*

Forces of Production and Biophysical Limits

While officially sanctioning a new understanding of global environmental change as largely anthropogenic, the *Welcome to the Anthropocene* video does not represent a fundamentally new narrative. In fact, it could be seen as the latest chapter in an older mainstream narrative, that of modern economic growth. Reflecting the contemporary hegemony of the gross domestic product (GDP) growth paradigm in global political economy (Schmelzer, 2016), the story of modern economic growth has featured in the education of generations of students in the post–world war two era (Barca, 2011). A Promethean tale, modern economic growth celebrates the increase of energy consumption and material production beyond the biophysical limits of renewable resources, overcoming what economic historians call the 'Malthusian trap' of the population/resources ratio. Such a tremendous leap forward – so the narrative goes – was brought about by the industrial revolution. Consequently, industrial growth is seen as the most relevant characteristic of modernity – what marks discontinuity with pre-industrial (reputedly pre-modern) economies, where production was largely based on solar and living energy.

Initiated in the early 1960s, the modern economic growth narrative reflected a widespread belief that a new historical age, the age of abundance, had finally opened for humanity due to the virtuous combination of two historical achievements of western Europe: 1) an enormous increase in labour productivity, achieved by tapping into the non-living energy of fossil fuels – that is, technological innovation and 2) an ability to turn this increased productivity into exchange value, thus reinvesting it into a new cycle of production – that is, capitalism. Mechanized industry, made possible by the coal-and-steam complex, facilitated an exponential increase in production and consumption per capita; economic liberalism, premised upon the enclosure and improvement of nature, allowed for the continuous expansion of mechanized industry and its social hegemony. The existence of a global trade system, already shaped by western capitalism since the 'long 16th century' (Moore, 2011a), allowed for the global expansion of industrialization.

By celebrating Europe's ability to break the circularity of the 'organic economy' (Wrigley, 1988) and reinvent the economy as an arrow pointing towards infinity (Raworth, 2017), modern economic growth is a tale of human liberation from nature – a liberation accomplished via industrial modernity. Energy use is the single most important carrier of this new meaning of modernity: more energy has been used globally since 1920 than in all of human history, and, in less than one lifetime (from 1950 to today), global energy use has multiplied by a factor of five (McNeill and Engelke, 2014: 9). Not by chance, the modern economic growth narrative started with, and is still largely repeated in, economic history accounts of energy (Kander et al., 2013): needless to say, fossil fuels play a fundamental and unique role in this liberation tale. Written by (mostly) white male academics sitting in ivy-league universities in the global North, these works reflect the (anti)ecological consciousness of industrial capitalism in the age of the Great Acceleration (Barca, 2011). Entirely devoted to celebrating the development of the forces of production, while cancelling the forces of reproduction out of historical agency, this is a master narrative literally speaking: a story told by the master in the colonial and patriarchal sense of the term – the head of the estate, the factory, the trade company; the owner of slaves and the holder of legal authority over women and animals. Modern economic growth is *his*tory: obliterating the social and ecological costs associated with fossil capital, it backgrounds the agency of the non-master subjects, and considers their sacrifice as inevitable and necessary to global historical progress.

From the 1990s onwards, the modern economic growth narrative has been interconnected with ecological modernization theory, which emerged as a response to the official recognition of a global ecological crisis on the part of the United Nations (UN) (Spaargaren and Mol, 1992). Based on a post-materialist sociological approach and on environmental economics (specifically, the Environmental Kuznets Curve), ecological modernization theory offered a positive and progressive view of the ecological crisis as one that could be solved by decoupling economic and material flows – separating wealth production from resource use and environmental degradation. It thus offered scientific support to discourses of sustainable development and green growth. Sustainability started to appear as an inevitable result of a technological fix, that is, the decrease of energy content per GDP unit, leading to a supposed dematerialization of the economy; and of a market fix – the commodification and financialization of nature, whose paramount translation into politics is the carbon trading market.

Like the modern economic growth narrative, ecological modernization postulated the universal validity of the experience of a few Northwestern European countries in the period of transition from an industrial to a post-industrial economic basis. With Western-centric progressive optimism, ecological modernization theory bypassed various problems of the Environmental Kuznets Curve: the fact that it is premised on shifting environmental costs towards third parties, namely 'developing countries' and the world's extractive frontiers; that the decrease in energy intensity per unit has led to an incremental growth in absolute production and consumption (the Jevons paradox); that trading in carbon emissions and other environmental services poses an insoluble moral problem – that of putting a price on nature, which reflects and reproduces social, spatial and species inequalities. All these problems are well-known and ecological modernization is a highly contested paradigm in the social sciences (White et al., 2016): nevertheless, it has become the dominant paradigm in global environmental politics, informing two global environmental summits (Rio 1992 and Rio 2012) and climate negotiations for the past two decades. Its ineffectiveness and inefficacy have now become evident; nevertheless we cannot get rid of it. It's a master's narrative that translates into a political dogma (Leonardi, 2017, 2019).

Most recently, ecological modernization theory has been incorporated within the Planetary Boundaries framework (Brown, 2017; Rockström et al., 2009), represented in the final chapter of the *Welcome to the Anthropocene* video. Although this framework is said to offer no guidance as to which policies are to be favoured to maintain human development within the prescribed 'safe operating space' (Steffen et al., 2015), the Stockholm Resilience Centre, which developed the framework, does offer policy advice and is a highly reputed contributor to the formulation of global environmental governance. The Planetary Boundary discourse adopts the language of Development Goals (now updated as Sustainable Development Goals – SDG), a paradigm that has been highly politicized and contested for several decades now (Death, 2010; Healy et al., 2015; Luke, 1995; Redclift, 2005); it thus implicitly endorses the Rio+20 'green growth' agenda, while ignoring (and thus silencing) all alternative visions and practices (Giacomini, 2018). The endorsement of a non-transformational approach is best understood when considering that the Planetary Boundaries concept originates from research on 'resilience'. As Sherilyn MacGregor (2017) has noted, 'the valorisation of climate resilience over human vulnerability removes expectations of citizen resistance to the root causes of ecological crisis, thereby casting it as an inevitable and therefore non-political fait accompli.'

Not by chance, the Planetary Boundaries framework has been adopted by the World Business Council on Sustainable Development (WBCSD), a forum of 200 'best-known brands in the world'[4]: these include transnational corporations

---

[4] See www.stockholmresilience.org/research/planetary-boundaries.html

that are responsible for 'double standard' practices in labour and environmental matters worldwide (Newell, 2012), even – in some cases – for widely recognized ecocide crimes, and that evidently find the Planetary Boundaries framework useful as a green-washing tool.[5] Before the 2012 Earth Summit, the WBCSD had lobbied with the International Chamber of Commerce and the Organisation for Economic Co-operation and Development through a UNEP-Business and Industry Global Dialogue aimed at 'providing the market-based solutions and practices that are essential to create a sustainable world'. The latter included a new framework for development financing linked to 'green economy' initiatives (Goodman and Salleh, 2013), thus laying the basis of what became the green growth strategy officially adopted at Rio+20. It soon became clear that this strategy was premised upon the further commodification of nature and financialization of the ecological crisis (Apostolopoulou and Cortes-Vazquez, 2018). In short, according to the Planetary Boundaries framework, no systemic change involving social structures and the global political economy is necessary; rather, sustainable development is still possible within ecological limits, and this can be achieved by spreading scientific and technological wisdom from Western industrialized countries to developing countries so they can adopt the best available options.

All this points to a paradox in the hegemonic Anthropocene narrative: by representing earth-system changes as the unintended consequence of Western civilization, in accordance with the master's narrative of modern economic growth, it maintains the validity of that story as one of progress which, as it happens, proceeds by trial and error, learns from its own mistakes and develops the tools by which those mistakes can be overturned. In short, the forces of production (science and industrial technology) are maintained as the only possible tool for understanding the errors and for repairing them. The system itself is not under question; its gender, class, spatial and racial inequalities are either invisible or irrelevant: no paradigm shift is necessary.

Growth: A Violent Narrative

The ecological modernization discourse can only function by hiding the social (human) costs of capitalist/industrial modernity – now abundantly documented by decades of research in environmental social sciences and humanities (Adamson et al., 2016; Bryant, 2015; Perreault et al., 2015; White et al., 2016). In their environmental history of the Great Acceleration, John McNeill and Peter Engelke (2014) document both the slow and the fast violence of

---

[5] The executive committee includes CEOs from Shell, Nestlé, Arcelor Mittal, Unilever and Sinopec. See www.wbcsd.org/Overview/About-us

capitalist/industrial modernity: the millions of deaths yearly due to air pollution related to fossil fuel combustion[6]; the long list of oil spills, gas flares and nuclear accidents, killing an undetermined number of people, both directly and via increased cancer rates for decades afterwards; the forty to eighty millions of marginalized peasants or Indigenous populations displaced by big dam constructions; and the appalling number of wars and nuclear bomb tests that have been quintessential to global GDP growth via military–industrial investments. They acknowledge the sacrifice of coal miners, oil drillers, women and all human and non-human life in mining areas, and the genocide of Indigenous peoples living on oil and natural gas frontiers, as well as the contamination of their territories (McNeill and Engelke, 2014).

Yet other dimensions of the violence of modern economic growth have been documented by scholars of industrial hazards and toxicity (Sellers and Melling, 2012): for example, the toll of pesticides and agrochemicals on workers' bodies and human lives in rural communities, consequent to the infamous (but still celebrated) 'green revolution'; or the asbestos and PVC tragedies that take place inexorably in working-class bodies even decades after occupational or community exposure. Environmental Justice scholars have documented the sacrifice zones created by industrial activities, and the disposable bodies that inhabit them, struggling to breathe while making their living through industrial toxicity (Armiero et al, 2019; Bullard, 2000); or the shanty towns where millions have been forced to live as a consequence of land grabbing and rural dispossessions, and the immense landfills where many seek sustenance as waste pickers (Davis, 2017; Medina, 2007). Migration scholars, for their part, have looked at mass migrations and their immense human suffering as intimately related to the environmental changes of the industrial era (Armiero and Tucker, 2017).

The celebration of fossil fuels as what made modern economic growth possible leaves no space for the acknowledgement of social costs, or their unequal distribution, with the effect of hiding the socio-spatial inequalities that are constitutive of capitalist/industrial modernity. Inevitably, the unequal distribution of the benefits of industrialization also disappears from view. Energy use is the most conspicuous example: as of 2013, 'the average north-American used about seventy times as much energy as the average Mozambican' (McNeill and Engelke, 2014: 10). Overall, the official Anthropocene storyline represents post-war globalization and the exponential increase in global GDP as the direct causes of a dramatic improvement in the living conditions of the vast majority of humanity, rather than its imperial one-

---

[6] Between thirty and forty million deaths have been attributed to air pollution between 1950 and 2015 – as high as the death toll of all wars around the world in the same period (McNeill and Engelke, 2014: 24)

third (Brand and Wissen, 2013). It is true, the story goes, that one billion suffer malnutrition, but the remaining six billion have never been more wealthy and healthy. The enormous income inequalities between rich and poor all around the world, which have been directly correlated to trade agreements and neoliberal austerity policies, and their continuous, scandalous rise over the course of the last three decades (Piketty, 2014) remain completely invisible.

As already mentioned, in the second half of the *Welcome to the Anthropocene* video the environmental costs of modern economic growth – global warming, loss of biodiversity, ocean acidification and other earth-system changes – are duly listed. It is the human costs of industrialization that the narrative refuses to acknowledge; it thus fails to account for the fact that social inequalities almost automatically translate into environmental inequalities, generating environmental injustice. The most macroscopic example is the fact that, also due to historical colonization and current indebtedness (Warlenius et al., 2015), extreme climate events are unevenly distributed across the planet and mostly concentrated in tropical and sub-tropical areas, which are among the world's poorest.

Representing industrialization as the explanation for anything good that has happened to humanity in the last 250 years, the Anthropocene storyline obliterates the agency of the forces of reproduction. The truly unprecedented growth in the world population in the twentieth century is implicitly attributed to capitalism's ability to sustain more people – completely bypassing the role of capitalist/patriarchal control over women's bodies as reproducers of cheap labour (Federici, 2004). Medical discoveries, and the average increase in the health and longevity of the world's population, are assumed to be a direct result of industrialization; no mention is made of the fundamental role of democratic and socialist forces in contrasting the degradation of life and labour under various industrial hazard regimes (Sellers and Melling, 2012). Similarly, agrochemicals are represented as the other key driver in population growth, obscuring the fact that half the world's population is still fed by family farming, fishing and gathering, largely via women's unwaged work[7].

To sum up the argument so far: the narrative violence of the official Anthropocene storyline transpires from the fact that it systematically silences both the structural inequalities of modern economic growth and the non-capitalist alternatives to it. While this master's narrative has been repeatedly challenged, it must be considered nonetheless as the hegemonic discourse underlying not only the official Anthropocene storyline, but (inter)governmental climate politics in general (Hamilton, 2015). Following this line of

---

[7] See www.fao.org/family-farming-decade/en/

reasoning, we can go further to consider the Anthropocene storyline as a form of realism similar to how Mark Fisher (2009) described capitalism in the post-socialist era, when the fall of the Soviet experience made many believe that history had come to an end and there were no alternatives to the capitalist order. Capitalist realism, according to Fisher, consists in 'the widespread sense that not only is capitalism the only viable political and economic system, but also that it is now impossible even to imagine a coherent alternative to it' (Fisher, 2009: 2). The *Welcome to the Anthropocene* story, I contend, might be understood as eco-capitalist realism: considering industrial growth as the only valuable form of human existence, it induces one to wonder how it can be saved by making it compatible with the earth's biophysical limits.

The Anthropocene as Eco-capitalist Realism

Never mentioned in the *Welcome to the Anthropocene* video (nor, for the most part, in the modern economic growth narrative), capitalist/industrial modernity is the true protagonist of the story. Along with science and technology developments, what the narrative celebrates is international trade, as incarnated by *globalization, marketing, tourism and huge investments*, which are depicted as bringing unprecedented wealth to a record number of people worldwide. The industrial revolution is represented as capitalism's coming of age in developing its technological and energy capacities, the forces of production, to the highest point in history; and the Great Acceleration as the latest chapter in capitalism's story, its mature phase, the full deployment of industrial power over the earth – geo-power.

Unlike previous chapters in the modern economic growth narrative, the official Anthropocene storyline does include consideration for what economists have called externalities, aka ecological degradation. Such an addition is justified by evidence of the enormity of modern economic growth's environmental impact upon the earth, and the consequent threat of ecological collapse. In this contemporary rendition of the narrative, ecological breakdown is seen as a troubling unintended consequence of ill-managing the geo-power of industrial capitalism, a power which humanity must learn to control and exercise within planetary boundaries. This is functional to carrying the message that industrial growth is necessary and beneficial to the well-being of humanity as a whole, and thus must be maintained in operation; what must change is the space for such operation to be safely carried out – a problem that only (Western) science and technology can solve. Enter eco-capitalist realism, or ecological modernization 2.0. What the video suggests, in fact, is not a critical reconsideration of the historical pattern which has led towards such an unprecedented threat, with the aim of identifying what was wrong with the modern economic growth model, but rather the possibility of finding a 'safe operating space' for this very model – not a different one. As in the ecological modernization discourse, its underlying message is not change but continuity.

This message is delivered through the video's format and language. Consisting of a single image, that of a revolving globe seen from space on which a graphic equation is superimposed, the video is a striking representation of the single most important driver of capitalist development: abstraction (Moore, 2011b). The equation appears to result from a combination of data about population and a list of environmental indicators (methane, carbon dioxide, nitrous oxide, tropical forest loss, domesticated land, energy use, atmospheric temperature, biodiversity loss, ozone depletion, nitrogen flux) mixed with a selection of ecological footprints (fisheries exploited, fertilizers used, rare earth extracted, urbanization, water use) and wealth indicators (number of motor vehicles and telephones, tourism, foreign investments) into a single line, rising at increasing pace since the late eighteenth century, and peaking after 1945. This homogenization of the world into a single numerical indicator reflects the logic and the graphic of GDP accounting, that is, encompassing *all that is* – production and destruction, living and non-living, private gains and social costs – through a principle of fictitious equivalence. The global ecological crisis becomes an equation seen from space by the all-knowing scientist who appears to be in control of the variables; ultimately, the crisis is assimilated to a problem of economic equilibrium, one which a global integrated science of ecology and economics might be able to solve.

This image is accompanied by a female voice with an inflexion recalling that of a children's bedtime storyteller: this is consistent with the educational character of the video, or better, with a certain understanding of what environmental education is about (Hutchings, 2014). The combined effect of picture and sound results in a subliminal message: that this constitutes a scientific, rational account of human history, carrying incontestable and value-free truth, which must be told in a simple language so that it can be absorbed by everyone. To fulfil its educational purpose, the Anthropocene story must be at once based on numbers while carrying a reassuring message about humanity's ability to make good use of science and technology to save itself.

The discursive *dispositif* of eco-capitalist realism has important implications for narrative justice, and for the politics of climate justice more generally. By taking capitalist/industrial modernity as its subject, the official Anthropocene storyline turns it into the only historically relevant form of socio-ecological relations on the global scale; this renders alternate perspectives of (and responses to) the planetary crisis invisible or irrelevant. Such a move is entirely consistent with end-of-history, post–cold war visions of how capitalism has conquered the world. After the fall of the Soviet system, moreover, socialist – or rather, centrally planned – industrial modernity (now chiefly represented by China) has tended to converge towards the capitalist model: this has increased its productivity, but also its inequality and its global environmental impact (Bond, 2019; Chertkovskaya, 2019). Historical convergence prompts the idea that the two systems' similitudes are more important than their differences, and that they form a unique historical bloc of industrial modernity with different grades of State regulation: as neither pure capitalism nor pure socialism have ever existed, the two systems should be seen as different, but also evolving, ways of organizing social metabolism (Martínez-Alier, 2002) around the common paradigm of modern economic growth.

From a narrative justice perspective, such claims make a lot of sense, as they are consistent with the lived experience of people and non-human nature on both sides of the iron curtain (Agyeman and Ogneva-Himmelberger, 2009; Kirchof and McNeill, 2019). Nevertheless, the historical relevance of the socialist model of industrial modernity does not coincide entirely with its State forms. Equally important, especially for those who found themselves living on the Western side of the cold war, has been the pressure that the Left (broadly intended as the variety of socialist movements and parties, labour organizations, as well as feminist and internationalist movements) has exercised upon capitalist/industrial modernity in order to make it compatible with social progress and the reproduction of life. From this perspective, it could be argued that *health, wealth, longevity and security* are not the result of global trade and capital, but of those forces which have opposed them via what can be described as 'the ecology of class' (see also the section 'Class' under 'Undoing the Anthropocene' below).

In the second decade of the twenty-first century, it has become increasingly evident that the ecological version of capitalist/industrial modernity officially adopted in Rio+20, and in all subsequent Conference of the Parties (COP) meetings, has translated into ineffective policies and that it is unquestionably failing the earth (IPBES, 2019; IPCC, 2019). The reason for this is not to be found in the narrative flaws of the official Anthropocene storyline, of course, but in the structural constraints of the global capitalist hegemony, and in the internal contradictions of the 'green growth' model (Hickel and Kallis, 2020; Parrique et al., 2019). Eco-capitalist realism has served the purpose of naturalizing this model as the only possible system of socio-ecological relations. It has literally made it 'easier to imagine the end of the world than the end of capitalism' (Fisher, 2009: 1) – and/or of GDP growth (Barca et al., 2019). As the global climate justice movement claims, a climate politics that wants to be effective must aim to change the system; clearly, though, such a system-change perspective cannot be based on the official narrative – it needs a new one.

The kind of information that is offered in educational projects is always a political choice, and, despite its pretence to constitute a scientific, value-free narrative, the *Welcome to the Anthropocene* video is no exception. In fact, abundant research has been produced in the environmental social sciences and humanities that, if considered, could have helped frame the Anthropocene storyline differently. Far from representing a path-breaking discourse, this narrative is consequent to and complicit with those of modern economic growth and ecological modernization, and its overall effect is that of naturalizing capitalist/industrial modernity by representing it as the only existential possibility for humanity. As the video's finale might suggest, the possibility is entirely open for human ingenuity and creativity to find technical solutions to replace failing earth-systems and lost biodiversity – to save human life without the need to save the rest of life as we know it. *Not just any human life, moreover, but life which is consistent with capitalist/industrial modernity.* It comes as no surprise, then, that the continuation of the highly industrialized, globally interconnected and hyper-consuming 'imperial mode of living (Brand and Wissen, 2013) is precisely what delegates at the Rio+20 conference, introduced with this video, declared to be 'the future we want'.[8] Such a tendency, it must be noted, is not unique to mainstream capitalist discourse, but is shared by a consistent tradition of thought on the anti-capitalist edge, and inspires a socialist version of eco-modernism. What is needed, therefore, is a radical anti-mastery rethinking of the discourse itself.

Undoing the Anthropocene

Undoing the Anthropocene master's narrative requires a critical analysis of its four levels of denial and backgrounding:

1. colonial relations: the only civilization that matters is Western;
2. gender relations: the only historical agency is that of the 'forces of production' (science, technology and industry);
3. class relations: social inequalities and exploitation do not matter;
4. species relations: the non-human living world does not matter.

Taken together, these different aspects of the Anthropocene master's narrative derive from the denial and backgrounding of the forces of reproduction, that is, those agencies – racialized, feminized, waged and unwaged, human and non-human labours – that keep the world alive.

---

[8] See www.un.org/ga/search/view_doc.asp?symbol=A/RES/66/288&Lang=E

While the master model of modernity is constitutive of capitalist/industrial modernity, it does not coincide with it entirely. On the one hand, capitalism adopted this model of rationality in reshaping the notion of modernity as the capacity to extract value from both human and non-human work; on the other hand, its key features (or part of them) can be also found in non-capitalist, that is, non-value oriented, social systems. State socialism as experienced in the Soviet bloc and China, or some of its post-colonial versions in Africa, Latin America and South-East Asia, have retained various historical combinations of coloniality/racism, heteropatriarchy/sexism and/or human supremacy/species-ism. Deeply ingrained politico-economic structures, from the local to the global scale, run counter to any attempt at dismantling the master model of modernity, so that a counter-master model has yet to be found in State formations. Yet, our best hopes for climate justice reside with it; thus we need to exercise a counter-mastery critique in every possible way to cultivate alternative, multiple and sustainable forms of modernity.

Race/Coloniality

Perhaps the most evident level of backgrounding of the Anthropocene master's narrative is that of coloniality. The story reflects what Plumwood (1993) considered the latest phase of mastering rationality, the devouring phase, in which the colonized world is 'appropriated, incorporated, into the selfhood and culture of the master, which forms its identity' (Plumwood, 1993: 41). This process engulfs the very definition of what is human, until nothing that can be recognized as such can exist outside of the master's identity. In the first phases, the colonized subject is implicitly denied human nature, which is only evoked for the purpose of asserting Western identity as fully human. In the final, devouring phase of master rationality, the Other disappears altogether from discourse and representation, insofar as the master 'seeks to create a slave-world, a "terra-formed" landscape which offers no resistance, which does not answer back because it no longer has a voice and language of its own' (Plumwood, 1993: 193).

From this perspective, we can consider the species-wide extension of the Anthropocene's *We* subject as a new chapter in the discursive formation of 'the West and the Rest' (Hall, 1992). This new chapter focuses on the industrial revolution as the entry point through which the non-Western has been able to finally enter Western modernity. As Gurminder Bhambra (2007) has demon-strated, the twentieth-century sociological imagination configured industrial-ization as constitutive of modernity, to the point that failing to industrialize was considered as failing to become modern (Bhambra, 2007). As a consequence, industrial wage-labour became the cornerstone around which modernized societies could address their social problems. In this sense, mainstream social thought has long contributed to the master model of modernity by relegating reproductive labours – those of women, peasants, Indigenous people and non-human work – to the sphere of the pre-modern, or even the anti-modern.

Like its economic history counterpart, this sociological imagination is also inherently racist. As Laura Pulido (2018) has argued, the Anthropocene storyline must be regarded as one uncritically incorporating – or rather *indifferent to* – racism. This is because, though largely absent from the Anthropocene narrative, racism was foundational to capitalist/Industrial modernity: this process, in fact, was premised upon characterizing indigenous peoples and their relational ontologies as uncivilized and inferior, akin to wild animals, in order to categorize the land that they inhabited as abandoned or empty, awaiting domestication and value extraction. At the same time, Black Africans were considered incomplete versions of the human, and their labour as legitimately available to whites. In this sense, the *We* subject of the Anthropocene storyline represents the ultimate version of racism, that in which the uncivilized Other has been devoured for its own benefit – assimilated into capitalist/industrial modernity. Consequently, the unified human identity is implicitly considered as a great historical achievement for *the Rest*, the final catching up of the undeveloped with the modern, fully developed subject, its exit from the state of immaturity (Dussel, 1993) and enter into the realm of history proper.

In the process, human identity, the Anthropos, comes to be conflated with the forces of production – and vice versa; paraphrasing Achille Mbembe, we can argue that civilization has been now conflated with industrial civilization, and the other-than-industrial (both Western and non-Western) is presupposed to be 'of lesser value, little importance, poor quality' (Mbembe, 2001); the world becomes a stage for the development of the industrial self, represented by the forces of production, and their mission of civilizational biopolitics. The *Welcome to the Anthropocene* storyline is not only consistent with this mainstream sociological narrative of modernity, but it takes it on a new level: that of planetary supremacy. Industrial modernity is naturalized as the end point of human evolution, and Anthropocene becomes the scientific, post-political term that signifies it.

Undoing the coloniality of the official Anthropocene storyline requires us to look at the climate and ecological crisis from a decolonial perspective (Davis and Todd, 2017). This is, in fact, the first fundamental step of a narrative project in the service of global climate justice. Alternate truths about capitalist/industrial modernity emerge from the work of Indigenous and Black authors: delinking themselves from the *We* subject and affirming their differential positionality face to industrialization and its socio-ecological consequences, they have produced a wealth of alternate stories that can guide us in the search for narrative justice. Many of these narratives allow us to not only criticize the coloniality of capitalist/industrial modernity, but also to see the recurring ecological, counter-entropic agency of the colonized, enslaved and racialized subjects of history.

As several authors have noted, a first way to counter the *indifference* of the Anthropocene narrative to coloniality and racism (Pulido, 2018) is to reject the idea of the industrial revolution as the entry point into the age of climate change, because this entry point discounts as irrelevant the process of original accumulation that allowed for capitalist/industrial modernity – a process in which Indigenous genocide and slavery constituted key components (Davis et al., 2019; Moore, 2016; Patel and Moore, 2018). The history of Black lives and labours, in particular, has shed new light on the making of capitalist/ industrial modernity through the plantation system that, from the sixteenth century onwards, took over colonial territories all over the world. A long time before the industrial revolution, the plantation already configured a master model of modernity based on white/capitalist hegemony over both human and non-human work. Its homogeneous, simplified eco-epistemes, built on slave labour and cheap energy – what Sidney Mintz (quoted in Sapp Moore et al., 2019) once termed 'a synthesis of field and factory' – form a large part of the Anthropocene landscape, and continue to expand to this day (Sapp Moore et al., 2019).

Based on a wealth of studies from Black scholars on the history of both plantations and 'counterplantations' (Casimir, 2010), which evoke the slaves' plot as a site for 'black ecologies' that call for a different understanding of humanness, Davis et al. (2019: 7) argue that decolonizing the Anthropocene narrative means to 'highlight liberatory acts that provide guidance for practicing a relational mode of being'. Key to black ecologies, the authors write, was the West African concept of 'good use' of the land as a source of both material and spiritual nourishment connecting people and non-human nature as well as different human generations, as opposed to the colonial imposition of Lockean visions of 'rational use' based on value extraction. This West African conception of the land points to the importance of recognizing the different humanities of the Anthropocene and their unequal relations of power.

Black narratives in relation to the history of food have revealed how crucial Black people's relation to the land was to grant the material and cultural reproduction of people, as well as a diversity of crops and nonhuman life forms.

African staples – including black eyed peas, okra, tamarind sorghum, millet, watermelon, rice, banana, and yam – adapted alongside food crops cultivated by Indigenous peoples in the Americas, provided sustenance in a plantation regime that was hostile to life that could not be commodified. Even if plantations were geared toward monocropping regimes of export-oriented commodity production, they were sustained by the cultivation of foods and animals practiced by enslaved peoples in the interstices, plots, and edges of plantations. (Davis et al., 2019: 8–9)

Not by chance, the nexus between liberation of both land and labour from value extraction is at the core of narratives like that of the *Nego Fugido* – a ritual of the Recôncavo region of Salvador de Bahia (Brazil) (Milanez and Pinto, 2017), that celebrates the struggles for liberation that the Black slaves from the Acupe sugar cane plantation enacted in the nineteenth century, and revives the memory of the community of *Vai-quem-quer*, which hosted rebels and fugitives in the mangrove swamp. Performing subsistence work was how Black people reclaimed the mangrove as a freed zone, a space liberated from capitalist/colonial control, while reaffirming their full humanity via an autonomous relationship with the land. This process initiated a long history of struggles on the part of the Quilombo communities to gain legal recognition of territorial autonomy as a form of compensation for their historical enslavement. In many cases, this history of commoning and autonomy has translated into a strenuous defence of ecological integrity against industrial contamination. Even when legally recognized, Quilombo territories are now surrounded by settler industrialism, and subject to violent attempts at dispossession and encroachment; the defence of the commons is thus a central element of Quilombo's political organization and community identity (Milanez and Pinto, 2017). Theirs is yet a different narrative of the Anthropocene, in which the advancement of capitalist/industrial modernity is resisted and countered via the joint struggle to liberate labour and the land from the grip of extractivism, commodification and ecocide.

Building on decolonial narratives, Donna Haraway and Anna Tsing have proposed that the Anthropocene be thought of as Plantationocene, the age in which, via colonization and slavery, 'radical, simplification; substitution of peoples, crops, microbes, and life forms; forced labor; and, crucially, the disordering of times of generation across species, including human beings' (Mitman et al., 2019) has taken over the world. Its legacy has been so naturalized that many people today believe this is the only way of farming. Plantation discipline, that is, has pushed other ways of farming to the margins of modernity. But illuminating the plantation background of the Anthropocene is also a way of acknowledging the agency of those historical subjects whose existence has been denied by the master model and yet was essential to it. In countering plantation discipline to keep themselves and their more-than-human communities alive, slave labour's agency has been one of the earliest and most enduring forces of reproduction acting within and against capitalist modernity.

Black, Latinx, Mestizx and Indigenous people's struggles for the commons and against industrial ecocide must be seen as the long-lasting historical forces that generated the US environmental justice movement and other anti-racist environmental movements all over the Americas (Escobar, 2008; LaDuke, 1999; Pulido, 1996; Taylor, 2016). In the Brazilian context, for example, quilombo's struggles are joined by those of other populations that the Brazilian constitution calls 'traditional' – chief among them are Indigenous groups. A powerful Indigenous counter-narrative of the Anthropocene comes from the public intellectual Ailton Krenak, from the Krenaki people of the Rio Doce valley in Minas Gerais, home to one of the greatest mining disasters in history (in November 2015).[9] In his latest book, *Ideias para adiar o fim do mundo* (*How to postpone the end of the world*), Krenak (2019) criticizes the modern concept of humanity as premised upon the idea that there is one right way of inhabiting the earth, carried out by an enlightened people, whose planetary hegemony is justified by its universal civilizational mission. He sees this hegemonic humanity, now represented by global institutions like the World Bank and the UN, as characterized by a false ecological consciousness, a pretence of being separated from and mastering its environment. He believes it is time to ask the question: 'why did we insist so much and for so long in joining this club [of humanity] that so much limits our inventiveness, creativity, existence and freedom?' (Krenak, 2019: 13). How can we justify this desire, he writes, when so many people have been deprived of the minimum conditions to exist, once modernization threw them off the land and out of the forests and 'into this blender called humanity' (Krenak, 2019: 14) where their place became the slums and their fate that of becoming a workforce? Clearly, the *We* that Krenak evokes is radically different from that evoked by the *Welcome to the Anthropocene* storyline: while his narrative acknowledges difference, and is devoted to making it visible, the former is devoted to annihilating it.

Sustainability, Krenak argues, must be seen as a fraudulent concept produced by this fraudulent humanity; it was invented to justify *their* assault on *our* conception of nature. *We* accepted it because 'for a long time, we got caught in this idea that we are humanity' and thus 'we got alienated from this organism to which we belong – Earth – and we turned to thinking that the Earth is one thing and we are another' (Krenak, 2019: 16). The only ones who found it vital to keep themselves clinging onto the land were those peoples (*Caiçaras, Índios,*

---

[9] See https://en.wikipedia.org/wiki/Mariana_dam_disaster

Quilombolas, Aborigines) that remained half-forgotten at the margins of the world. Krenak calls them the *sub-humanity* – a 'gross, rustic organic layer' that is clearly distinct from the 'cool humanity' that predicates itself upon separation from the rest of the natural world (Krenak, 2019: 22). Adopting the perspective of this other humanity, he claims, leads one to liberate citizenship from the consumerism that now pervades it – an idea he attributes to José Mujica[10] – to redefine it as 'alterity', namely, 'being in the world in a critical and conscious way', and 'living in a land full of meanings, a common platform for different cosmovisions' (Krenak, 2019: 25): an ability he attributes to the Yanomani people, as recounted by their shaman Davi Kopenawa (Kopenawa and Albert, 2013).

Krenak's narrative speaks directly to the Anthropocene storyline and its hegemonic *We*. He suggests that *postponing the end of the world* has everything to do with contesting the homogeneous vision of humanity, a leverage point from which to condemn and reject the kind of world that the UN wants to save, while building alliances with various peoples who are struggling for a world where bio/cultural diversity is respected and celebrated as foundational to the polis.

This is no wishful thinking, but political theory based on unique historical praxis. Defined as 'one of the greatest political and intellectual figures [to have] emerged from the Brazilian Indigenous movement since the end of the 1970s' (Viveiros de Castro, 2015), Ailton Krenak was a member of Brazil's constituent assembly after the fall of dictatorship and a key figure in the struggle for the institution of 'extractive reserves', a groundbreaking system of protected areas that considered people and the forest as a whole. He was a close friend of rubber tapper unionist Chico Mendes, with whom he formed the Alliance of the Peoples of the Forest, a coalition representing the great diversity of the Indigenous and rural population of Brazil (Cohn, 2015; Hecht and Cockburn, 2010). Emerging from those struggles, the principle of *florestania* (literally, forest-zenship) translates the diversity principle into a concrete utopia, filling it with political meaning: that the forest and its peoples constitute a polis, a more-than-human community endowed with proper political subjectivity and equal entitlements (to preservation and a decent life) as the rest of the nation (Barbosa de Almeida, 2008). Following centuries of racist discrimination, dispossession and violence, *florestania* meant that the Indigenous and peasant populations of

---

[10] José Alberto 'Pepe' Mujica Cordano (b. 1935), President of Uruguay from 2010 to 2015, has been described as 'the world's humblest head of state' due to his austere lifestyle and his donation of around 90 per cent of his $12,000 monthly salary to charities. The story of his imprisonment during Uruguayan dictatorship is narrated in the movie *A twelve-year night* (*La noche de 12 años*) by Álvaro Brechner. See https://en.wikipedia.org/wiki/Jos%C3%A9_Mujica

Brazil were equal citizens entitled to the same rights as whites and urban folk, rather than inferior others who needed to conform to the hegemonic model of humanity, or else be sacrificed to national progress.

In short, Krenak's reverse Anthropocene narrative explains why Indigenous and Quilombo (Afro-descendent) populations have taken on the attribute of 'traditional', re-signifying it as the right to cultivate an autonomous way of being *within* modernity. Struggling for the value of diversity, Krenak concludes, is the way in which the Indigenous peoples of Brazil have resisted and survived the end of their world for the last 500 years, each struggle helping to push the falling sky up again and breathe anew (Kopenawa and Albert, 2013).

The dialectic between environmental violence and resistance to it under colonial and postcolonial rule is also at the core of Indigenous environmental narratives from North America. From the very first lines of her book *All our relations,* for example, Dakota writer and activist Winona LaDuke (1999: 1) fleshed out an alternate Anthropocene storyline by claiming: 'The last 150 years have seen a great holocaust. There have been more species lost in the past years than since the Ice Age. At the same time, Indigenous peoples have been disappearing from the face of the earth.' Massacred, cheated and robbed of their land, LaDuke wrote, the Indigenous peoples of North America (i.e. their bodies/territories) had become 'subjects to the most invasive industrial inter-ventions imaginable' (LaDuke, 1999: 3), their reservations being targeted for toxic and radioactive waste disposal, coal and uranium extraction, the siting of heavy industry (and its dumps) and nuclear bomb testing. Having documented how the industrial mode of production destroyed native American life tribe after tribe across the USA and Canada, LaDuke noted how Western science and Indigenous knowledge were converging in recognizing the ecological crisis, albeit on very different grounds. She mentioned a 1998 gathering of NASA scientists with Indigenous elders to discuss global warming, in which the response the scientists received was something akin to 'You did it, you fix it' (LaDuke, 1999: 197). She read this episode against the grain of different ways of looking at the past trajectory – ultimately, to different narratives of the crisis. In the indigenous narrative, ecological crisis has been caused by a history of legal/political/cultural subordination to the interests of industrial corporations, a history in which 'the "common good" has been redefined as "maximum corporate production and profit". ... Corporations have been granted the power of "eminent domain" and the right to inflict private injury and personal damage when pursuing "progressive improvements" '. (La Duke, 1999: 199)

A classic North American environmental justice narrative, *All our relations* shows how, far from being value-neutral tools for human progress, Western science and industrial technology (aka the forces of production) have been part and parcel of the global history of capitalist geo-power. They have become the master's tools. The connubium, celebrated by the modern economic growth narrative, between Western technological ingenuity and capitalist institutions, is precisely what LaDuke's narrative considered to be the problem. It was the corporate mastering of science and technology that, in her account, had led Indigenous environmental movements to distrust it as part of the solution to the ecological crisis, and to look instead towards the path of spirituality, intended as a political principle – namely, the defence of the commons for the sake of seven generations to come.

Seen through Indigenous eyes, modern economic growth ceases to be a triumphalist account of human (qua Western) exceptionalism and becomes a history of environmental violence, whose dreadful consequences are not projected into a dystopian future, but have been already experienced by many human and non-human generations. As Kyle Whyte (2017: 209) has noted, Anishinaabe people today live in the dystopian future of their ancestors, in what he calls 'the fallout of settler industrial campaigns', which 'both dramatically changed ecosystems, such as through deforestation, overharvesting and pollution, and obstructed Indigenous peoples' capacities to adapt to the changes, such as through removal and containment on reservations'. In the view of Anishinaabe, industrialization is associated with settlement – a white/colonial type of social relation to the land – and consequently with the colonial/nation State and its politics of spatial segregation. This is key to a recognition of how, as Whyte again writes: 'Indigenous peoples have long advocated that the conservation and restoration of native species, the cultivation of first foods, and the maintenance of spiritual practices require the existence of plants and animals of particular genetic parentage whose lives are woven with ecologically, economically and culturally significant stories.' (Whyte, 2017: 207). Whyte mentions several projects of Anishinaabe restoration and conservation of traditional staple food, such as sturgeon and wild rice, and of water (*nibi*) habitat integrity that 'learn from, adapt, and put into practice ancient stories and relationships involving humans, nonhuman species, and ecosystems' (Whyte, 2017: 213). This resonates with the reading that Arturo Escobar (2008) has given of Afro-Colombian environmental conservation practices as expressions of what he calls an ontology of thinking–feeling (*sentipensar*) with the earth, emerging from struggles for 'territorial difference'. By adopting the detached scientific overview of resilience and planetary boundaries, the official Anthropocene narrative misses completely the radical difference of these decolonial political ecologies that point to embeddedness with place and more-than-human relationality as long-standing practices of countering extinction.

To summarize: the official Anthropocene storyline represents a devouring Western rationality built upon the denial/backgrounding of colonialism and of Indigenous and Black history. This discursive *dispositif* manages, at once, to deny historically unequal responsibilities for climate change (and thus historical 'climate debt' of the colonizers towards the colonized), and to represent such fictitious equalization as 'development' – as a historical achievement for the colonized. Decolonial narratives of the current epoch show how the flat ontology of humanity vs nature which underpins the *Welcome to the Anthropocene* storyline misses completely the point that *We*, capitalist/industrial modernity, has been defined through the exclusion of racialized peoples and their ontologies from the realm of humanity proper, and that the ecological crisis has emerged from the annihilation of alternate possibilities of inhabitation of the earth. To the video's authors, and to the UN bureaucrats who adopted it, Indigenous and Black histories are completely irrelevant to understanding the 'interactions between humans and the planet' in the current age. Conversely, colonization, enslavement and racialization, as well as trade agreements and other globalization disasters, simply *do not matter* as intrinsic components of the modern world, which appears as what needs to be saved and sustained – rather than changed. This shows how the master's narrative of eco-capitalist realism can only work by backgrounding the other-than-master subjects of history.

Applying a decolonial and materialist feminist lens to the Anthropocene storyline allows us to make visible the work of the colonized (slaves, Indigenous and racialized subjects) who have taken care of people and the land all along – the denied and backgrounded part of the modernity/coloniality project (Mignolo and Walsh, 2018). In fact, accounting for the unequal geographical distribution of ecological responsibilities and ecocide is only one way of conceptualizing ecological debt. Another way is to account for what capitalist/industrial modernity and all who live in it owe to Black and Indigenous people for the work and the knowledge they have devoted to keep the world alive – for their forces of reproduction. The next section will offer a detailed analysis of this concept as it emerged in the 1990s from materialist ecofeminist critiques of the patriarchy/capitalist/colonial nexus, and has become embedded in decolonial feminist struggles for the integrity of the earth/body/territory (Cabnal, 2010) today.

Sex/Gender

While the *We* subject of the official Anthropocene storyline is intended to be gender neutral, this discursive neutrality has the effect of keeping the sexism that is constitutive of capitalist/industrial modernity well hidden within the narrative. Since the mid-1970s, ecofeminism has developed invaluable analytical tools to reveal how ecological crisis and hetero/patriarchy are related to each other in complex ways. Like all militant/intellectual projects, ecofeminism is traversed by debates and critical scrutiny because it incorporates different traditions of thought and praxis; the most relevant to my argument is that of materialist ecofeminism, which developed from the feminist critique of political economy.

This new approach had emerged from within and around the Wages for Housework (WfH) campaign, that spread across Italy, the UK and the USA in the early 1970s. The campaign was based on the claim that capitalism was deeply entrenched with the appropriation of unpaid reproductive labour (James, 2012). As Selma James and Maria Rosa Dalla Costa explained, women produced the basic capitalist commodity, labour power, yet they did not receive wages for this work. Theirs was the wageless work that created the conditions for the reproduction of industrial society. This lack of recognition of the economic value of women's work underlay two interrelated problems of capitalist/industrial modernity: women's subordination to men, and the subordination of reproduction (or life making) to production (or industrial growth). The proper political response could not be to push women into the labour market – a push that capitalism itself was interested in, due to the wage differential with men. 'Women refuse the myth of liberation through work', Dalla Costa and James claimed (quoted in James, 2012: 59). Instead, the key demand of the WfH campaign was that reproductive work should be compensated – rather than appropriated for free – so that women could put limits and boundaries on it, while at the same time obtaining the financial power that would allow them to both refuse waged work and be independent from male control.

Most importantly, this refusal was seen as consonant with the refusal of *development* as a response to colonialism in the Third World. It was not the capitalist valuation of their work that could liberate women and colonized people, but autonomy and self-determination. Over the following decades, the movement demanded that compensation for reproductive work should be funded via public money, ideally diverted from military expenses, and brought this demand to various levels of government and to the UN; it finally converged with degrowth and Green New Deal campaigns in demanding a care income 'for people and planet' (James and López, in press).

Building on the connections that the WfH movement had posed between sex, race and class struggles, some feminist scholars and intellectuals – we can call them materialist, or socialist, ecofeminists – put nature and ecology into the equation. They linked the politico/economic devaluation of reproduction with the degradation of the environment, thus producing a radically new narrative of capitalist/industrial modernity. A widely recognized foundational reference for materialist ecofeminism is the work of German sociologist Maria Mies, and, in particular her book *Patriarchy and accumulation on the world scale* (1986). Mies claimed that feminism needed to go beyond the analysis of reproductive labour in Western countries, connecting it with the specific material conditions of women on the peripheries of the capitalist world system, in order to identify 'the contradictory policies regarding women which were, and still are, promoted by the brotherhood of militarists, capitalists, politicians and scientists in their effort to keep the growth model going' (Mies, 1986: 3). This can be seen as the basis for a decolonial/feminist ecosocialism, premised on the rejection of GDP growth as a universal measure of progress (Gregoratti and Raphael, 2019).

Developing this perspective, Mies wrote, required rethinking the concepts of nature, labour, the sexual division of labour, the family and productivity: in short, it required a feminist critique of political economy. The latter had conceptualized *labour* in opposition to both nature and women, that is, as a male-coded, transcendent agency actively shaping the world by giving it value. As a consequence, the labour of producing life (in the sense of giving birth, nurturing and raising human beings) was not seen as 'the conscious interaction of a human being with nature, that is, a truly human activity, but rather as an activity of nature, which produces plants and animals unconsciously and has no control over this process' (Mies, 1986: 45). According to Mies, a hierarchical dualism between surplus-producing labour (within the market) and life-producing labour (mostly, but not only, outside the market) translated into the definition of women and their work as 'nature'. On the contrary, she claimed, all the labour that goes into the production of life must be called *productive* 'in the broad sense of producing use values for the satisfaction of human needs' (Mies, 1986: 47).

Mies's overall argument was that the production of life, or subsistence production, performed mainly in unwaged form by women, slaves, peasants and other colonized subjects, constituted the material possibility for 'productive labour' to be raised and exploited. Being uncompensated for by a wage, its capitalist appropriation (or 'superexploitation', as she termed it) could only be obtained – in the last instance – via violence or coercive institutions. In fact, she wrote, the sexual division of labour was built upon neither biological nor purely economic determinants, but on the male monopoly of (armed) violence, which 'constitutes the political power necessary for the establishment of lasting relations of exploitation between men and women, as well as between different classes and peoples' (Mies, 1986: 4).

From the sixteenth century onwards, starting with the witch hunt, The basis for capital accumulation in Europe had been laid upon a parallel process of conquest and exploitation of the colonies and of women's bodies and productive capacities. Only after this regime of accumulation had been established through violence, could industrialization begin. With it, Mies argued, 'science and technology became the main "productive forces" through which men could "emancipate" themselves from nature, as well as from women' (Mies, 1986: 75). At the same time, European women from different social classes (including those participating in settler colonialism) were subjected to a process of 'house-wifization' – they were gradually excluded from political economy, intended as the public space of progress and modernity-building, and secluded into 'the ideal of the domesticated privatized woman, concerned with "love" and consumption and dependent on a male "breadwinner" ' (Mies, 1986: 103).

Mies' work should not be considered an isolated voice, but one resonant with other materialist ecofeminist scholars writing between the 1980s and 1990s. Among them, the groundbreaking work of Carolyn Merchant must be mentioned here. Following her widely cited *The death of nature*, which recounted the scientific revolution as a gendered process largely based upon patriarchal violence (particularly via the witch hunt), Merchant's (1989) *Ecological revolutions* constituted a highly original contribution towards an ecological and feminist approach to history: it remains probably the study that most clearly illuminates the ecological implications of colonial/heteropatriarchal/capitalist modernity. Designed to explain radical socio-ecological transformations that occurred at a regional scale, that of New England from pre-colonial times to the twentieth century, Merchant's ecological revolutions are radical changes occurring simultaneously in the relations between production and reproduction and between production and ecology, with the effect of radically transforming the habitat, population and social relations. The book showed how both colonial and industrial capitalism were premised upon a reconfiguration of gender relations, leading to the submission of life-producing to value-producing labour.

A third, vital contribution to the development of an ecofeminist narrative of capitalist modernity came from Federici's *Caliban and the witch* (2004). A Marxist/feminist intellectual and activist, Federici offered an in-depth study of how, in early modern Europe, the female body had been remade 'into an instrument . . . for the expansion of the workforce, treated as a natural breeding-machine, functioning according to rhythms outside of women's control' (Federici, 2009: 49). This new sexual division of labour, she argued, had redefined proletarian women as natural resources, a sort of commons open to appropriation, for the sake of improved productivity. Capitalist patriarchy was born: due to the parallel enclosure of land, women gradually lost access to means of subsistence and, since their work had been removed from the sphere of the market, they became economically dependent on men. With a movement similar to that used in respect of natives in the colonies, Federici argued, European women were sub-humanized in law, enslaved in the economy and subject to the genocidal terror of witch-hunting. Together with colonization and the slave trade, the war on women thus formed a substantial step in the emergence of the Anthropocene, as it granted the steady provision of cheap labour (Moore, 2016) that would facilitate industrialization. As this was a generalized process concerning all women (although, obviously, in different forms), Marxist feminists see it as a de facto redefinition of the female sex into a class – that of reproductive labourers.

Contributing to this body of thought, the Marxist ecofeminist Mary Mellor (1996) offered a first conceptualization of the 'forces of reproduction': the 'underlaboring work that women do that is incorporated into the material world of men as represented in the theoretical framework of historical material-ism' (Mellor, 1996: 257). Historical materialism, she claimed, should break free from the artificial boundaries of productivism, by which 'women's lives become theoretically a leftover category, the "sphere of reproduction" ' (Mellor, 1996: 260), resulting in devastating ecological impacts – such as those registered in 'command economies'. Rather than being ignored or denied, Mellor argued, women's bodies should be understood as the material basis upon which specific social relations were imposed, namely, as forces of reproduction that had to be organized through 'relations of reproduction' (Mellor, 1996: 261).

At the same time, feminism allowed women to take advantage of their specific standpoint to produce an alternative, non-dualist view of the world, overcoming the nature/society dichotomies typical of Western thought. The transcendence of Western politico-economic categories has allowed ecofemin-ists to see modern economic growth as a process by which some humans get liberated from scarcity at the expense of other humans and the non-human world. This suggests that a feminist version of ecosocialism would allow for the reconstruction of society on egalitarian principles while also respecting the autonomous agency of the natural and our interdependency with it.

From this theoretical standpoint, materialist ecofeminists have advocated for a thorough reconsideration of economic value. In *Globalization and its terrors*, for example, Teresa Brennan (2003) revisited Marx's theory of value, pointing to how products and services exchanged on the market required the input of living nature (human and non-human). Not only labour, she wrote, but nature as well gives more than it costs; capital transfers the cost of the reproduction of both labour and nature upon third parties – women, colonized and racialized subjects. The hidden results of this process – beyond the visible circuit of money – are the sickened bodies (and territories) where toxic waste gets disposed of, and the extra labour that is needed to take care of them. From the Marshall Islands (De Ishtar, 2009) to the Niger Delta (Turner and Brownhill, 2004), and through countless other stories, ecofeminist activists and scholars have pointed to how illness and death in the Anthropocene are the effects of a highly industrialized/militarized model of progress, whose costs have been largely borne by 'women, nature and colonies' (Mies, 1986). As Ewa Charkiewicz (2009) notes, excluded from the production of value, 'women are included in the economic and political on condition that they fulfil caring duties'. Along with *patria potestas*, that is, the father's right to kill, she argues, sovereign power is premised upon *cura materna* – the feminine duty to care, which translates into their prevailing responsibility for reproduction, 'absorbing social costs of the global war on living nature' (Charkiewicz, 2009: 83).

Embracing this perspective, Ariel Salleh (2009: 4–5) has proposed the concept of 'embodied debt' – the debt that societies owe to unpaid reproductive workers for their contribution to regenerating the conditions of production, including the future labour force. This debt, she argues, should be seen as interlocked with two others: the 'social debt' owed by capitalists for the surplus value extracted from workers through both waged and unwaged labour (e.g. that of slaves); and the 'ecological debt' owed by colonial to colonized countries for the plundering of their natural resources. This approach, which the author calls *embodied materialism*, allows for the development of a materialist ecofeminist narrative of the Anthropocene: one that sees the ecological crisis as arising from the interconnection of the three forms of theft operated by a global system of exploitation.

Embodied debt points to the fact that subsistence farming and gathering, as well as care for both urban and rural environments, are forms of unpaid reproductive work that complement domestic work in granting the conditions of production. Salleh defines this work as meta-industrial: surrounding, and granting the conditions for, industrial work. This approach complements and expands the concept of social reproduction – domestic labour and human care – with that of *environmental reproduction*, that is, earthcare labour. Environmental reproduction could be theorized as the work of making non-human nature fit for human reproduction while also protecting it from exploitation, and securing the conditions for nature's own regeneration, for the needs of present and future generations. Environmental reproduction, according to Salleh, is guided by a principle of eco-sufficiency (rather than eco-efficiency) – a non-extractive relation to non-human nature as a provider for human needs rather than profit. She posits eco-sufficiency as the true response to climate and ecological debt: if accompanied by financial debt cancellation and adopted globally, it would imply halting the continuation of extraction in poorer countries and their possible recovery from ecological degradation, allowing them to 'keep oil in the soil'[11] and to develop local autonomy and resource sovereignty.

Lacking scholarly legitimization, Salleh notes, the eco-sufficiency approach is virtually ignored in expert consultancies on environmental policy. The reason is not simply cultural, of course, but also structural: its adoption would require 'a commitment to annual reductions in resource use by industrialized nations' (Salleh, 2009:18), similar to what some now call degrowth, thus threatening the neoliberal growth economy. From a feminist perspective, Salleh argues, degrowth could also mean liberation for the industrial working classes of the world – for sex/gendered and racialized wage-labour trapped in a system of productivism and consumerism. The ecofeminist perspective, in fact, points to the need not simply to reduce industrial work (as in the degrowth discourse), but to reverse the hierarchical subordination of meta-industrial to industrial work that characterizes both capitalist and State-led economies in the political economy of growth.

As reproductive labourers, women in capitalist modernity have not only embodied, but also counteracted ecological contradictions: they have, as a feminist saying goes, organized resistance from the kitchen table (Fakier and Cock, 2018; Merchant 1996, 2005). This allows conceptualization of the alternate agencies that are inscribed *within and against* capitalist modernity, and particularly around a politics of the commons. Materialist ecofeminists have seen women as the primary defenders of the commons because these constitute the material basis for reproductive work: this perspective allows us to see the defence of common access to, and preservation of, natural and built environments (soil, water, forests, fisheries, but also air, landscapes and urban spaces) as a form of labour resistance against dispossession and degrading conditions of reproductive work. This would explain why women worldwide have been at the forefront of urban farming, tree-hugging and tree-planting actions, anti-nuclear and anti-mining mobilizations, opposition to destructive megaprojects, water privatization and toxic landfills, and similar actions (Federici, 2009; Gaard, 2011). Carolyn Merchant (1996) called this agency *earthcare*. Many have criticized this as an essentialist claim, spurring a debate, as Christine Bauhardt writes, 'around the uncomfortable nexus between nature, care for others and about the environment, and the sex/gender relation' (Bauhardt, 2019). It is important to remember, however, that, as she notes, 'At issue is the practice of care labour and not an essentialising of the female body' (Bauhardt, 2019: 27).

---

[11] See for example: https://movimientom4.org/2016/01/la-vida-en-el-centro-y-el-crudo-bajo-tierra-el-yasuni-en-clave-feminista/

Materialist ecofeminists also insist that women must be recognized as comprising the vast majority of the global reproductive and caregiving class, both historically and at present. They point to the fact that women form the large majority of the global proletariat (i.e. of the dispossessed and exploited of the world) – a class of labourers whose bodies and productive capacities have been appropriated by capital and capitalist institutions. From this perspective, women's environmental agency can be understood as that of political subjects who reclaim control over the means (and conditions) of re/production: their bodies and the non-human environment. In other words: if the nexus between women and non-human nature as co-producers of labour power has been socially constructed through capitalist relations of reproduction, then women's environmental and reproductive struggles are to be seen as part of the general class struggle. For socialist ecofeminists, this requires disavowing the paradigm of modern economic growth, because the latter has subordinated both reproduction and ecology to production, considering them as means to capitalist accumulation.

This can be considered a very basic tenet of materialist ecofeminism: as Mary Mellor (1996: 256) puts it, 'by separating production from both reproduction and from nature, patriarchal capitalism has created a sphere of "false" freedom that ignores biological and ecological parameters'; a truly ecological socialism must reverse this order, by subordinating production to reproduction and ecology (Merchant, 2005). Faced with the catastrophic dimensions of the current ecological crisis, recent developments in social reproduction theory and the global feminist movement indicate concrete possibilities for assuming this perspective (Arruzza et al., 2019; Batthacharya, 2017; Fraser, 2014). In fact, the Global Women's Strike has evolved from a struggle over domestic work to one that includes the work of earthcare that capitalist/industrial modernity has externalized onto women and other backgrounded/feminized subjects, thus challenging capitalist/industrial and military violence to radically transform productive and reproductive relations.[12]

Materialist ecofeminism configures as an invaluable tool for political subjectivation; however, it should not be taken as a generalized claim about women, but rather as a critical analysis of material relations of re/production that have generated specific political responses, and that create new political possibilities in the present. The colonial/capitalist sexual division of labour, with its ferocious normativity, has oppressed and continues to oppress too many

---

[12] See https://globalwomenstrike.net/open-letter-to-governments-a-care-income-now/. This vision was also adopted by the Italian section of the movement (*Non Una di Meno*), as expressed in their programmatic plan: see https://nonunadimeno.files.wordpress.com/2017/11/abbiamo_un_piano.pdf

generations of women across the world to be ignored as a powerful driver towards liberation. Of course, many women have subscribed to the master model of modernity and progress, buying into lean-in feminism and uncritical consumption patterns and aspirations, or accepting their 'housewifization' and dependence on the male wage. Like all historical subjects, women make choices, even if these stem from conditions not of their choosing. The same applies to the male workers that historical materialism has traditionally considered capital's grave-diggers. As Mellor (1996) again noted, talking about reproductive labour and its ecological potential is no more essentialist than talking about industrial labour and its revolutionary potential: rather, it means recognizing the historically determined conditions in which (most) women stand in the global division of labour, acknowledging the specific ways in which labour and gender have been made to intersect in capitalist modernity, and refusing to comply with deeply ingrained understandings of domestic and subsistence work as unproductive or passive.

Moreover, materialist ecofeminists have long recognized that, although subsistence work is predominantly carried out by women, this is for historical and social, not biological reasons, and that men in peasant and Indigenous communities, and even in industrial economies, also perform reproductive, care and subsistence labour. Due to 'subconsciously displaced sex/gender attitudes' Salleh (2009: 9) writes, politicians, scholars and activists are prevented from identifying this counter-entropic work and grasping its social value. The same perspective is shared by most materialist ecofeminists: after the Zapatista uprising of the early 1990s, for example, Maria Rosa Dalla Costa (2003) – another prominent figure in social reproduction theory and the feminist movement of the 1970s – advocated for a broader understanding of earthcare which was not limited to women's environmental agency but included peasant and Indigenous movements in their struggles for food sovereignty and for the commons.

Over the past three decades, two interlinked bodies of scholarship – feminist ecological economics and feminist political ecology (FPE) – have built upon, or critically incorporated, the basic principles of materialist ecofeminism (Buckingham-Hatfield, 2000; Harcourt and Nelson, 2015; Perkins et al., 2005; Rocheleau and Nirmal, 2015). Stemming from Marilyn Waring's idea of feminist accounting (Waring, 1999), a number of analytical and normative concepts have emerged from feminist ecological economics (Nelson and Power, 2018), such as sustainable provisioning (Nelson, 1993; Pietilä, 2006), sustaining production (Gowdy and O'Hara, 1997), caring economy (Jochimsen and Knobloch, 1997), re/productivity, (Biesecker and Hofmeister, 2010), *wellth* economics (Mellor, 2019) and *carefull* community economies (Dombroski et al., 2019).

FPE, on its part, has offered invaluable critiques of development and conservation policies from the perspective of 'the complex interactions among class, race, gender, ethnicity, sexuality, and the environment in terms of rights, responsibilities, knowledges, and social movements' (Rocheleau and Nirmal, 2015). Rather than focusing on women as a general category of subsistence providers, FPE tends to see gender as one among several social constructs that determine socio-natures (Nightingale, 2006). Overall, responding in self-reflective and creative ways to critiques of essentialism, and countering systematic silencing on the part of mainstream environmental/social science, scholars in feminist ecological economics and political ecology have developed important conceptual tools for foregrounding the existing and possible 'alternatives to hegemonic development processes' (Bauhardt and Harcourt, 2019: 13).

More recently, FPE has shown how, tied to subsistence and care tasks, actively discriminated against, subject to violence and threats, women and lesbian, gay, bisexual, transgender, queer, and intersex+ (LGBTQI+) people around the world – especially those who are Indigenous, rural, Black and/or working class – have been disproportionately vulnerable to climate and ecological hazards (Gaard, 2015). Starting from the analysis of gendered climate inequalities, FPE then moves to question 'the highly militarized, masculinized, centralized, and corporate-driven responses to climate change ... calling on the mainstream and progressive Left scientific communities to redress the historical and contemporary exclusions of feminist analysis' (Rocheleau and Nirmal, 2015: 17). It calls into question climate governance and discourse that sees women and other 'vulnerable subjects' as either victims or heroes of resilience (Di Chiro, 2017; MacGregor 2017), and even mainstream representations of the earth as Mother Nature (Tola, 2018), which ultimately subject it to oedipal desires of domination on the part of a hegemonic masculinist subject (Salleh, 2016). In other words, FPE shows how the gender/climate nexus is far more complex and layered than a simple women-as-victims problem; in fact, applying a gender lens to climate discourse and politics allows one to see them as an expression of hegemonic (eco-modern) masculinity (MacGregor, 2017).

The concept of hegemonic masculinity, put forward by transgender scholar Raewyn Connell (1985), has helped to clarify that there exist different possibilities of expressing masculinity, and that dominant forms emerge from struggles for hegemony in different contexts (Messerschmidt, 2018). Capitalist/industrial modernity can be seen as coinciding with a hegemonic form, industrial masculinity, that stems from Western colonialism and hetero-patriarchy, adding to it an unprecedented capacity to produce wealth via the exploitation of fossil fuels and the mechanization of production. As such, industrial masculinity has been profoundly enmeshed with the ecological crisis. Over the past two decades, by merging with ecological modernization theory, industrial masculinity has generated a new hegemonic model – eco-modern masculinity (Hultman, 2017). By privileging the forces of production as the key historical agency of the last 250 years, the Anthropocene storyline reflects this eco-modern masculinity, insofar as it hides and discounts as irrelevant the agency of reproductive subjects and the other-than-industrial ways of interacting with the biosphere.

From a feminist, decolonial and climate justice perspective, addressing the global ecological crisis requires questioning the hegemonic eco-modern masculinity of the Anthropocene. Gender studies offer invaluable instruments to do just that. Building on the path-breaking work of Judith Butler (1990, 2004), for example, we can see how, just like gender, the Anthropocene is a social construction, that is, a concept that attributes to nature (the human species) what should, in fact, be attributed to society (the master model of modernity). Just as gender does not coincide with sex, so Anthropocene agency does not coincide with that of humanity: they are made to coincide by a mastering discourse that wants us believe that the only truly human identity is a master/ industrial identity – the others being aberrations or incomplete versions of the human. By naturalizing this particular version of humanity, modelled on the white male subject who masters nature and the less-than-human others via the forces of production, the official Anthropocene narrative operates as the equivalent of a surgeon who modifies the genitalia of the non-binary newborn: it reduces the possibilities of human existence to a dualist alternative between pre-defined identities. Performing capitalist/industrial modernity becomes the equivalent of performing *humanity*: the performance can be improved, but the script and the acting subject remain the same. Nonetheless, like male/female, the humanity/nature dualism is false; humanity is not a separate identity vis-à-vis nature (in fact, it is made from it), and it can manifest in different forms and be performed in different modes of relationship with the web of life.

A hybridization of the ecofeminist tradition with queer thought has been developed by some scholars and activists into an approach called 'queer ecology'. For Greta Gaard, this means acknowledging that 'the reason/erotic and heterosexual/queer dualisms have now become part of the master identity and that dismantling these dualisms is integral to the project of ecofeminism' (Gaard, 1997, quoted in Bauhardt, 2019: 28). Referring to Plumwood's work, Gaard sees climate change and homophobia as linked 'in the reason/erotic dualism of the Master Model' (Gaard, 2015: 29). She concurs with other feminist political ecologists that climate change, 'may be described as white industrial-capitalist heteromale supremacy on steroids, boosted by widespread injustices of gender and race, sexuality and species' (Gaard, 2005: 27).

Consequently, climate discourse and politics can only be transformed through queer, feminist and post-humanist perspectives, as exemplified by the Principles of Climate Justice formulated in Bali in 2002,[13] which included categories of gender, indigeneity, age, ability, wealth and health.

Building on this perspective, Christine Bauhardt (2019: 29) calls for a delinking of the normative tie between sexuality and motherhood in order to understand generativity 'as a web of biological, social and cultural dimensions'. Such claims resonate with Donna Haraway's (2016: 102) invitation to 'Make kin, not babies!', and with current struggles for reproductive rights within the global feminist movement to grant women full autonomy over their bodies, rejecting heteronormative social drives to re/produce the labour force and objectified socio-natures, disentangling reproduction from its ties with productivism and the mastering/commodification of non-human nature. This inherent nexus between queer and ecofeminist politics seems to have become widely accepted in both ecological and feminist movements, which are now calling themselves ecotransfeminists.[14]

'Making kin' starts from the assumption that, if generating new life is still a prerogative of female bodies, this by no means implies that parenting (nurturing and socializing children) should be female-only work to be performed within the nuclear hetero family. In fact, femaleness and reproduction should be seen as in a non-exclusive relationship, as female bodies are not necessarily productive, or they may choose not to reproduce themselves, or reproduce on behalf of others. Moreover, reproduction is certainly a more-than-human affair in the sense that the human body is part of a transcorporeal web of ecological interrelations that affect its reproductivity, and vice versa (Alaimo, 2010), and reproduction may involve or require bio-technical tools. At the same time, 'making kin' is an invitation to go beyond rigid separations between the human and other species, practising love and affect in extended communities of care, with important implications for earthcare. In fact, earthcare and environmental reproduction work can be performed by people of different sex/gender identification, as demonstrated, for example, by the long-standing vegan and anti-speciesist engagement of queer and lesbian activists (Sandilands, 2016). Moreover, earthcare is also always a more-than-human affair, involving the interaction of human with non-human forces.

---

[13] See https://corpwatch.org/article/bali-principles-climate-justice

[14] See, for example, in Spain: https://ecopolitica.org/ecoloqueersmo-parte-iii/ and https://paraisoin terespecie.com/principal/transfeminismo-antiespecista/; in Italy: https://nonunadimeno .wordpress.com/2019/01/29/seminaria-2-giornate-ecotransfemministe-verso-lottomarzo/ and https://retecorpieterranud.wixsite.com/seminaria/blog/siamo-ecotransfemministu-antispecistu-perch%C3%A8

What do 'queer ecologies' tell us about the forces of reproduction, then? Seeing the Anthropocene as a gendered concept uncritically reflecting the heteropatriarchal order helps us to not only criticize its inherent coincidence with hegemonic masculinity, but to go beyond sex/gender binarism itself, illuminating the backgrounded agencies of people of all sex/gender identification as actual and potential forces of reproduction. This allows us to rethink the forces of reproduction from non-binary and also more-than-human perspectives: they start to be seen as not simply coinciding with the colonized and feminized unpaid work of producing and caring for life, but as a collective of earthcare composed of all those subjects who are engaged in resisting the master version of modernity by countering the subordination of life to social imperatives of production/accumulation.

This brief and somehow approximate sketch gives us a glimpse into the pathbreaking possibilities implicit in queering the forces of reproduction, as well as of the theoretical complexities involved. A major point of tension is provided by the different visions of agency (whether this should be extended to objects) and, related to this, of technology in general. New materialism tends to see human agency as inherently incorporating technology, which cannot be separated from it, but rather should be embraced in the more-than-human understanding of subjectivity. Materialist ecofeminism, however, tends to see technology as a dangerous and often violent social *dispositif* of control over human and non-human life. Clearly, there are shortcomings on both sides, which cannot be exhaustively addressed here. However, the political potentialities of a coalition between the two are worth the challenge (Casselot, 2016): at stake is the possibility of providing formidable tools for dismantling the Anthropocene master's house.

It is imperative to add that this challenge can only be addressed from a decolonial standpoint, by acknowledging the relevance of Latin American decolonial feminisms, first theorized by Maria Lugones (2010). She wrote:

> As Christianity became the most powerful instrument in the transformative mission [of colonialism], the normativity that tied gender and civilization became involved in the erasure of community, of ecological practices, knowledges of planting, weaving and the cosmos, and not only in changing and controlling reproductive and sexual practices. One can begin to appreciate the ties between the colonial introduction of the instrumental concept of nature central to capitalism and the colonial introduction of the modern concept of gender. (quoted in Walsh, 2015:112)

Decolonial feminism has allowed us to see that, while Indigenous and Mestizx peoples appear to have often transgressed the heteropatriarchal norms of Christianity, they have also incorporated them with pre-existing forms of patriarchal oppression from ancestral cosmogonies, and how this process has entailed new social constructions of both gender and nature.

Referring to the work of Lorena Cabnal, Julieta Paredes, Betty Ruth Lozano and others, Catherine Walsh argues that the Indigenous and communitarian feminisms of Abya Yala are 'challenging the idealization of gender duality, parity, and complementarity' and 'present-day simplification and recuperation of these principles by men as mandates to control, order, define, and subordinate women' (Mignolo and Walsh, 2018: 41). A very similar move is taking place in the Middle East via Kurdish feminism's Jineoloji theory (Piccardi, 2018). What these 'feminisms otherwise' (Lozano, quoted in Mignolo and Walsh, 2018: 41) have in common is a struggle for the defence of the inextricable nexus between human and non-human natures, territory and collective rights. Acknowledging this represents an important move in twenty-first-century ecofeminist thought, which allows recovering and *rethinking with* early critiques of the nexus between 'women nature and colonies' in materialist ecofeminism.

In the past decade, a new, decolonial wave of ecofeminist movements has been emerging in Abya Yala as a response to the 'commodity consensus' (Svampa, 2019) mandated by neoliberal globalization and the eco-capitalist turn. One of their most important contributions is the idea of earth/body/territory (*territorio/ cuerpo/tierra*), originally put forward by Lorena Cabnal (2010), as the organic material unit that is politically interpellated by extractivism (Colectivo Miradas Críticas del Territorio desde el Feminismo, 2017; Espinosa et al., 2014; Guillamón and Ruiz, 2015). Like the Zapatistas and the Aliança dos Povos da Floresta mentioned in the section 'Race/Coloniality' above, these insurgent social movements have been speaking not only to their own countries and people, but to (and on behalf of) humanity. Their voice is collective and political, but also internally differentiated and mediated by allied subjects – mostly, engaged academics and public intellectuals from Latin America and elsewhere.

As Kyran Asher (2017) has noted, this poses the unavoidable problem that Gayatri Spivak called the 'aporia of representation'. Silvia Rivera Cusicanqui has also warned us against the cooptation of Indigenous intellectuals on the part of white academia, coming at the price of their disconnection from the – sometimes untranslatable – languages and cosmovisions of their own people. In fact, decolonial representations might end up hiding the agency of Indigenous women in processes of political mobilization and transformation of the State; and academic feminism risks sticking to a vision of domestic labour as exclusively feminine, while refusing to engage with Indigenous configurations of work and gender, thus producing an essentialized vision of Indigenous cosmovisions – invariably ancestral and immutable. Responding to these important critiques is a vital challenge for decolonial ecofeminism, and it invites us to exercise vigilance by keeping in mind how all nature–cultural configurations take shape 'within specific conjunctures of political economy, state policies, and cultural politics' (Asher, 2017: 523).

One issue now seems clear, however: that women from peasant, Afrodescendent, mestizo and Indigenous groups are at the forefront of anti-extractive resistance across the world (Oxfam International, 2019). A number of decolonial feminists from Latin America tell us that women are framing this as part of a broader decolonial, anti-capitalist, cosmopolitical and anti-heteropatriarchal struggle for the radically otherwise, engendering new under-standings of Indigenous and peasant movements as subjects of an alternative vision of modernity and a prefiguration of an alternative common sense (Millán Moncayo, 2011). What decolonial feminisms represent, I argue, is the insur-gence of an ecofeminist struggle against not only capitalist extractivism but the entire master model of hegemonic masculinity, uncritically incorporated by self-proclaimed socialist and decolonial elites in Abya Yala, which identify human progress with the development of the forces of production.

Several decolonial feminists, for example, have exposed how governments in Ecuador and Bolivia have practically disavowed the Pachamama principles incorporated in their constitutions by pursuing extractivist and eco-capitalist policies and harshly persecuting those who oppose them, deeming them as irrational, infantile and feminine (Bravo and Moreano, 2015; Tola, 2018; Walsh, 2015). This speaks to the overall argument of this Element – that undoing the hegemonic Anthropocene storyline requires, simultaneously, that all four axes of master rationality are addressed. Undoing the Anthropocene thus becomes a necessary step within a project of *naturcultural* liberation: that of renegotiating the Anthropos beyond male/female, nature/culture and pro-ductive/reproductive dualisms, enabling us to reject the master's model of modernity as the only possibility for a future human coexistence on planet Earth.

Class

Although the *We* subject of the Anthropocene storyline is meant to be classless – or, its message is that social inequalities and exploitation do not matter to the ecological crisis – much historical evidence tells us that this is not the case. Even (or perhaps, precisely) by accepting the English industrial revolution as the starting point of this new epoch, it is impossible to disregard the fact that industrialization was predicated upon and reproduced social inequalities via private ownership of the means of production – a process known as the making of the working class. In this sense, the Anthropocene concept represents the ultimate depoliticization of the ecological crisis, obscuring 'the fact that the forces directing the destruction of nature and the wealth produced from it are owned and controlled overwhelmingly by an unaccountable, mainly white, mainly male elite' (Plumwood, 1993: 12). On the contrary, taking class into account begins with the recognition that the factory system that lay at the core of 'fossil capitalism' (Malm, 2016) would not have been possible without a combined process of world-scale proletarianization of the workforce, that is, its forced separation from the means of production via what I have called the 'enclosure and improvement project' (Barca, 2010), or capital's war against the commons.

The long history of primitive accumulation demonstrates how the true enemies of capitalist/industrial modernity are subsistence production, food sovereignty and autonomy, based on the direct relationship of people with non-human nature; thus, capital's first objective was turning commoners into prole-tarians (Caffentzis and Federici, 2014; De Angelis, 2017; Harvey, 2003; Linebaugh, 2014) in order to create 'the background conditions for exploitation' (Fraser, 2014). This process, which continues to take place in the never-ending global expansion of commodity production, has resulted in the separation of town and country and forced concentration of the dispossessed in urban centres and/or industrial activities, initiating the entropic process that Marx – and today's eco-Marxists – called 'metabolic rift' (Foster, 2000). The latter is understood as a rupture in the metabolic interaction between people and their natural habitat, from local to global scales: examples are the disruption of the global carbon cycle and the flooding of atmospheric carbon sinks; or the chemical degradation of soils due to mechanized farming (Clark and Foster, 2009; Clark and York, 2005). Although metabolic rift is a planetary process related to the global extension of capitalist modernity, its effects tend to concentrate in what environmental justice scholars have called 'sacrifice zones', and to bioaccumulate in the human and non-human bodies that inhabit them – or the 'organosphere' (Armiero and De Angelis, 2017). By breaking down the commons and commoning relationships among humans, and between them and the rest of the natural world, capitalist modernity creates *waste* relationships, or the unequal distribution of waste along lines of social differentiation.

In short: from a historical-materialist perspective, the working class, or proletariat, and metabolic rift originate from a unique, global process of violent separation of people from their means of subsistence, which also disrupts the biosphere. The ecological crisis is thus a direct consequence of class making. The significance of this for our understanding of the Anthropocene is becoming clearer beyond the circle of eco-Marxist thought.

Since capitalist modernity has naturalized class and other inequalities as necessary evils that allow for the supposedly greater common good of economic growth, it has tied working-class survival to the infinite expansion of the forces of production, including the production of waste (Schutz, 2011; see also Schnaiberg, 1980). Seen from a class perspective, concerns with mass consumerism – very common within the environmentalist tradition – appear as partly misplaced, because they tend to hide the fact that the overconsumption of cheap commodities is the effect of deeper root causes: one of importance is the alienation of labour, which pushes waged workers to seek personal fulfilment elsewhere, rather than through their work (Koch, 2019; Schutz, 2011). Countering alienation should thus be seen as a fundamental moment of working-class oriented ecological politics (Roelvink, 2013). This, however, must be complemented by another structural character of class society: it is not only commodity consumption but also, and more fundamentally, social welfare that depends on GDP growth, making working-class people especially vulnerable to environmental trade-offs.

Turning commoners into proletarians, however, does not automatically imply that they all become waged workers. On the contrary, capitalist societies function by maintaining part of them as an unpaid labour class that provides for the reproduction of waged workers and of the system as a whole – what feminist political economy calls social reproduction (Bhattacharya, 2017; Ferguson, 2019). Materialist ecofeminists have theorized this 'hidden abode' as one that takes place at world scale, and includes non-human nature. According to Silvia Federici (2009: 59), for example, capitalist modernity created 'a global assembly line ... that cut the cost of the commodities necessary to produce labour-power in Europe'. This line linked the exploitation of waged workers to the appropriation of the unpaid work of women and slaves, aimed at allowing for the sustenance of the working class while keeping wages as low as possible. This process, she noted, made waged workers dependent on (and often complicit in) the appropriation of unpaid work through the sexual and colonial divisions of labour and – to a great extent – the destruction of nature. Mies, Merchant, Salleh and other materialist ecofeminists have all insisted that the capitalist separation and re-articulation of 'productive' and 'reproductive' subjects within a global chain of exploitation constitutes the structural cause of the ecological crisis. Building on this scholarship, Jason Moore (2016) has, more recently, redefined the concept of 'unpaid work' as the ensemble of human and non-human energy expenditure in the production of life outside the cash nexus.

An ecologically aware notion of capitalism must not only rely on expanded notions of labour and value but also, crucially, should lead to a corresponding expansion of the notion of working class. Feminist theorists have greatly contributed to this endeavour, by turning the concept of class into a dynamic process of interrelation among various forms of social differentiation – intersecting waged and domestic, formal and informal work with the social production of race, gender, (dis)ability, space and the body itself – and tracing all these back to the differential valuations that characterize capitalist society (Acker, 2006; Gibson-Graham et al., 2000). Rather than taking class as a predetermined category, this scholarship allows for discussion about class-making as a historical and spatial process. What needs to be better understood, however, is the environmental dimension of class-making, that is, how working-class subjectivity meets ecology.

Since the 1990s, environmental justice (EJ) movements and scholars have amply documented how the environmental costs of capitalist modernity, and of industrialization specifically, have unequally affected people and places along intersecting lines of socio-spatial differentiation (Agyeman, 2014; Bullard, 2000; Harvey, 1999). It is now well understood that race, gender, ethnicity, age, ability and place are all – in varied ways – mixed in the production of environmental inequalities (Pellow, 2000), which tend to concentrate along the expansion lines of global social metabolism (Martínez Alier, 2002).[15] This body of knowledge contributes in fundamental ways to broadening our understanding of class-making as inherently linked to environment-making. Here, I want to explore this nexus further, asking the questions: How are ecology and class related to each other? How is the Anthropocene embedded and embodied in working-class communities? Whereas EJ points to the unequal distribution of pollution across society, affected communities are typically looked at as forces that resist the production process from outside. Workers and the labour process, as well as their resistance at the point of production, rarely figure in these accounts.

The history of industrial hazards shows how the toxic embodiments of the Anthropocene (Cielemęcka and Åsberg, 2019; Roberts and Langston, 2008) are not only transcorporeal and transpecies, but they are also intersected by class difference in the web of systemic, material and symbolic relations between working-class people and their habitats, that is, their living and working environments. Stories coming from the sacrifice zones of industrial modernity show how, embodying the ecological contradictions of both capitalism and State socialism, workers and their communities develop specific forms of ecological consciousness. The latter, however, is mediated by the different forms of both paid and unpaid work that sustain and reproduce the working-class community

---

[15] See also www.ejatlas.org

in and beyond the workplace itself, including social and environmental reproduction (Barca and Leonardi, 2018).

Materialist ecofeminism helps us see the ecology of working-class communities as particularly shaped by the sexual division of labour. This has given men the role of breadwinners, making them bargain for wages that heavily discount their health and safety, or accept job blackmails that compromise the health and safety of entire communities and their territories; and it has assigned women the role of reproducers and caregivers, but also of economically marginal and/or dependent subjects, with little or no bargaining and decision-making power in society. In other words, economic dependency on industrial work, typically experienced by working-class communities, is correlated with a material and symbolic devaluation of meta-industrial work. Since the economic system considers life-making as valueless, people become dependent on value-making activities (thus, on industrial wages) for their survival. This, in turn, generates job blackmails – the corporate practice of threatening industrial workers with a choice between employment and environmental/public health (Kazis and Grossman, 1982) – thus deeply impairing people's ability to react to the depleting and degrading effects of metabolic rift on their territories. All this makes industrial workers subject to an unsustainable contradiction, which they embody physically and mentally: that between their social role as value-makers and breadwinners, and their embeddedness in life-making and in socio-ecological interrelations that are typically harmed by industrial production. 'Staying with the trouble' (Haraway, 2016) of this contradiction between production and reproduction is the stuff that makes lives in working-class communities.

A specialized literature now tells us about the ecology of working-class communities in many sacrifice zones around the world (e.g. Bell, 2013; Mah, 2012; van Horssen, 2016; Ziglioli, 2016). While male breadwinners, insensitive to ecological and health concerns, and female reproducers, subordinated and secluded within the unpolitical sphere of domestic labour, are the stereotypical categories that populate mainstream media accounts of the working class, both research and working-class self-representation tell us different, infinitely more nuanced and complex stories. Poetry, creative writing, drama, (auto)biography, reportage and cinema (see, for example, Seger, 2015) have created working-class narratives of the Anthropocene.

In this vein, I will let the working class speak for itself through the voice of a worker/poet, Ferruccio Brugnaro (b. 1936). His voice comes to us from the now abandoned petrochemical area of Porto Marghera – a material effect of 'the cannibal mechanism of the development narrative' (Iovino, 2016), whose immense, lifeless skeleton still lingers over the city of Venice. Brugnaro's artistic career developed in the 1960s when, as a union activist, he started distributing short novels, poems and texts on cyclostyle around the factories and at unions' schools (Mueller, 2015). His poems (Brugnaro, 1997) give us illuminating glimpses into working-class ecological consciousness, as this is made out of transcorporeal relations (Alaimo, 2010) between the worker's body, a built environment made of concrete, steel and unruly flows of unnamed poisons, and the non-human lifeworld; his work shows us how this transcorporeality is mediated by work, social position and political agency.

> Giant cement blocks / huge iron scaffoldings / long pipes / are camped in my blood. / Dust, iron and asphalt / have covered my entire soul. / My eyes are heavy / with thick, poisonously yellow / mushroom clouds / pressing directly against the sky.

And soon after:

> What I'm hearing in my flesh is / long siren-wails / armor-plated shrieks / cutting noises. / The smoke-stacks are wounds, deep / craters open / on my body. (*Non ditemi di non disturbarvi*) (Brugnaro, 1997)[16]

But it is not just the worker's body that is affected here: the local ecosystem, its air, soil and water, are equally affected by industry, and with them the entire lifeworld. Brugnaro's poems take place under a dark, turbulent sky where 'the body of the earth wobbles on a thin loop of steel without light nor voice'. Here, one day 'the air smells of rotten eggs / it's infected / by tetraethyl hydrocarbons, / tar'; he picks-up a bird from the asphalt, 'a tiny bird / grey and red / all shivering / its eyes almost shut / and its beak full / of greenish foam'. The bird, he thinks, must have eaten some grains of sulphur, or perhaps some other poison, from the same ground where he walks. 'I've heard it begging / my hand / with hardness', he adds (*L'ho sentito implorare con durezza*) (Brugnaro, 1997).

The material, life-and-death interdependencies within working-class ecology become unmistakably clear when the normal, slow violence of industrial contamination that takes place silently day by day, bursts out in sudden accidents.

> Purple smoke everywhere, smoke / dust in huge clouds. / A chemical unit / has blown out / in the night. / It's raised like a mushroom cloud / I don't know how many fellows / workers / have been / suffocated / scorched. The town is in anguish / stricken more than by a thousand / bombs, / terrified. / The people are all / one long / cry / that's scratching every stone / scratching / every tree / biting hard into the earth / and sky / a long / never-ending cry. / Listen, listen. (*Nella notte è esploso un reparto*) (Brugnaro, 1997)

---

[16] This and the following quotations are my own translation from the Italian version of the poems.

Being one with a damaged environment and with its people, the worker cries for recognition, for society at large to acknowledge the industrial dust and the poisons as its own, rather than someone else's – a cry for re-embeddedness. The harm done to any working-class community is a harm done to the common lifeworld, and society must take responsibility for it.

> Don't you people tell me not to call on you / not to bother you / Don't tell me to leave you alone. Death is working like a dog / against life. Death is laid bare. / Don't you people tell me it's none of your business. (*Non ditemi di non disturbarvi*) (Brugnaro, 1997)

Most of all, these poems give us a sense of the immense disillusionment and the unbearable bitterness experienced by industrial workers once it becomes clear to them that their sacrifice has brought about death – that the bare life (Agamben, 1995) of factory workers, the heroes of industrial modernity, has turned into *bare death*. In Brugnaro, this awareness combines with the experience of factory dismissal, bringing about the sense that an entire epoch – the dream of progress and emancipation – is now over, that all is left is a mud lake: 'Our greatest dream / is wandering stunned and blind / around / an immense lake / of mud. Our time now is / far / far / off' (*Il nostro tempo*) (Brugnaro, 1997). It also entails a sense of loyalty, a longing for solidarity with those workers still facing the monster:

> I drag myself along the factory / walls / day and night. / I'm always by these walls. / I can't help it / I can't go away. / Many comrades I have inside there / alone, amidst the phosgene / before the horrible / stoke-holes. / I just can't detach. / My heart is in there / my struggle / burning high / like a torch towards the future. (*Non posso staccarmi*) (Brugnaro, 1997)

The poet's sense of camaraderie is made stronger by his knowledge of workers being on the frontline of an atrocious, deeply deceitful war:

> Enough with the emphysemas / with the intoxications / with the systematic / silent destruction. / Enough with this atrocious war / waged in the factories / in the name of humanity / of progress, of love. / Enough. / Our blood / is fed up. (*Basta con questa atroce guerra*) (Brugnaro, 1997)

Facing death daily by the industrial machine, workers cannot but embody ecological consciousness. Under a 'coughing, red-faced sun' and yellowish clouds dense with sulphur dioxide, one day they rise up. On this day, 'the sky and the earth happily witness' an immense workers' assembly gathering by the factory walls. Together, workers raise a far, unmistakeable cry: 'Pack-up all your plants / your progress / we don't want death. / Take death away from here immediately' (*L'assemblea di fabbrica*) (Brugnaro, 1997).

In Brugnaro, ecological consciousness turns the old-time workers' struggle against the masters into something new: this time they are not striking for better wages, but to defend life itself:

> We have walked out of our switchboards and stations. / We have walked out of all our units. / We struck hard today. / We want to strike hard. / Under a sun not seen before / now thousands and thousands of us / are circling life. / Life today with all the endurance / of our wounds / of our anguish / is pressing once and for all / its foot of fire down upon death. (*Basta con questa atroce guerra*) (Brugnaro, 1997)

Time-honoured workers' struggles at the point of production are reclaimed, in Brugnaro, as a tool for something new: taking the commons away from the master's grip, or getting rid of the masters once and for all:

> We don't want masters anymore / of any kind. / They've already splashed around too much / in our blood / already feasted plenty / on our lives. / Don't make so many questions / just look at our wounds / the wounds of peasants / of miners. / This plant must be yanked out of the world / once and forever.

And further:

> We don't want masters anymore / because the masters / are all the same / because they want the earth / all for themselves / because they want the sun / all for themselves / because they steal, they trample / they never stop / because they kill, they kill / day and night under the sky. (*Non vogliamo più padroni*) (Brugnaro, 1997)

The natural world outside of the factory walls, beyond the city's smoky skyline, is not just a sympathetic witness to the workers rising up, but rather it speaks to them through the poet. The bird that Brugnaro finds on the ground speaks to him sensorially, through the hardness of its agonizing body in his palm, and the message the poet gets is one of endurance, the survival imperative of resisting death:

> Inside my hand / I have touched / silently / all the pain / the extinguishing / and the excruciating / inexorable / living. / I have discovered / resistance / stubbornness / secret and crazy / that won't submit. (*L'ho sentito implorare con durezza*) (Brugnaro, 1997)

The sky over Porto Marghera also gives him a message of hope, of struggle for a better future:

> There's a star / Maria / tonight / so clear and big / like the struggle that the exploited / are waging / now in the world. . . . It's beautiful / like the earth that we're making. (*C'è una stella, Maria, stasera*) (Brugnaro, 1997)

Working-class community ecologies around the world show us how the metabolic rift of capitalist modernity has profoundly remade the 'organosphere' (Armiero and De Angelis, 2017), that is, the inextricable assemblage of people's bodies, communities and environments. Working-class poetry gives voice to a kind of ecological consciousness that is profoundly different from much of the middle-class or mainstream environmentalist discourse. First, there is a clear awareness that there is no going back to an enchanted world, that life will have to be reconstructed through struggle, a struggle in which workers need to take part. Second, saving the environment has everything to do with saving working-class lives themselves. Third, there is no salvaging the world within the current system. For people and the environment to be safe, the masters of industry will have to let go of their grip over the lifeworld, and leave.

In some cases, recognizing that environmental injustice is not a natural fact but the result of social inequalities has led working-class communities to overcoming the division between labour and environmental organizing, and to struggle for a radical transformation of the economy, based on principles of mutual interdependency between production, reproduction and ecology (Barca and Leonardi, 2018). For the most part, these stories have yet to enter the official, progressive narrative of the Anthropocene; in fact, most accounts of environmental (in)justice tend to omit the messy reality of working-class communities, their contradictions remaining unexpressed, their wounds laid open to political instrumentalizations and job blackmailing.

A key actor in this alternate scenario of environmental consciousness and mobilization has been labour environmentalism, that is, the environmental agency of trade unions and labour organizations. A number of studies have documented how political consciousness of the environmental and public health costs of industrialization has been formed in the workplace, and is physically embodied by working people in their daily interaction with the hazards of production. This in turn invites a reconsideration of the active role that workers in the post-war era have played in shaping modern ecological consciousness and regulation, both within and outside (even, sometimes, against) their organizations: promoting a number of important legislative reforms, struggling for the improvement of work environments, demanding the extension of workplace health and safety regulations to society as a whole. This method of struggle in labour environmentalism had been made possible, in different historical moments, through the political alliance between trade unions and environmental organizations – an alliance that is constantly threatened by changes in the political and economic scenario.

Labour environmentalism has developed all along the Anthropocene, acting as a necessary and healthy antidote to metabolic rift. It has undergone two historical phases. The first, centred on the connection between occupational, environmental and public health, reached its peak in coincidence with the adoption of Fordist policies in industrialized countries. This is what Italian political ecologists in the 1970s called the 'ecology of class'. It is exemplified by union mobilizations that took place in different parts of the world during the Fordist era: well-known cases are the Australian Green Bans against urban development and gentrification (Burgmann and Burgmann, 1998), the boycott against pesticides by the United Farmworkers in California and the political engagement of the Oil, Chemical and Atomic Workers that led to the Clean Air and Clean Water Acts in the USA (Montrie, 2008).

The second phase of labour environmentalism, starting after the Brundtland declaration (1987) and the first Earth Summit (Rio 1992), has been centred on the concept of 'sustainable development'; it probably reached its peak at the second Earth Summit (Rio 2012), where major trade union organizations undersigned the official declaration on the need for the adoption of 'green growth' policies at the global level. This second phase testifies to a growing political consensus on the need to tackle climate change, which has brought greening of the economy centre stage while encouraging union mobilization on environmental matters as part of a broader social agenda. This process has generated tremendous opportunities but also tensions in labour environmentalism. The International Trade Union Confederation (ITUC) and the International Labour Organization (ILO) have adopted a rather reductive version of Just Transition (JT) – which centres on the demand that the post–carbon transition should not be paid for by workers through job losses and the destabilization of local communities. This vision reflects a masculinist and Western-centric bias that persists in most large trade union confederations (even when they are led by women), focusing on blue-collar jobs in heavy industry and infrastructures as the only sectors worth defending and 'greening', while downplaying the crucial contribution of agriculture, domestic and social reproduction work.

If, however, we look at labour environmentalism on the ground – below the meta-level of national and international confederations – we do find stories that carry profound meaning and hope for a true ecological revolution. One such story can be found in the Amazon forest within the Brazilian state of Acre, home to the *seringueiros* (rubber tappers), a population made up of landless workers who had migrated to the area from the poorer northeast region, after extensive agrarian dispossessions in their home regions, to work for the 'rubber barons' in the early twentieth century. In the early to mid-1980s, through a newly formed grassroots union movement (harshly persecuted by Brazil's then dictatorial regime), the *seringueiros* organized a series of landmark struggles to defend the forest from timber companies and from the 'rubber barons' who, faced with falling profits, planned to increase exploitation with unsustainable costs for the workers and the forest alike.

By the end of that decade, the *seringueiros* had become known worldwide due to the assassination of their leader Chico Mendes a few years before the first Earth Summit in Rio de Janeiro in 1992. Following Mendes' vision, the *seringueiros* continued to pursue their battle, joining protection of the Amazon forest, now understood by global public opinion as a planetary resource, with social justice and labour emancipation in their communities. Seeing the Amazon as their living and working environment, their source of livelihood and cultural identity, the workers defended it as a commons. Eventually, they won the battle and a new form of conservation unit – called an 'extractive reserve' (Resex) because it allowed for the sustainable extraction of non-timber forest products – was passed into law. Organized into formal associations, the *seringueiros,* along with other workers who joined the Resex, obtained the right to live and work in the forest commons for their own benefit, with legal protection from external encroachment. They had managed to get rid of their masters. Inspired by Indigenous communities' way of life and formulated in collaboration with environmental activists and academics, the 'extractive reserve' is a major contribution that this movement has made to keeping both the Amazon and its people alive (Barca and Milanez, in press).

The rubber tappers' story tells us that labour environmentalism can have truly profound, revolutionary effects; however, in the *seringueiros'* experience, this came at a high price. Mendes's killing was only one among a long list of assassinations, systematically planned and executed in the past three decades, along what Brazilian political ecologists have called the 'arc of deforestation' (*arco do desmatamento*). The latter is now rapidly advancing deep into the core of the Brazilian Amazon due to the increasing global demand for soy, meat, energy, timber, iron, aluminium and other commodities (Milanez, 2019). Defending the forest from this powerful drive for accumulation is a terrifying, life-threatening task – one that has taken too many lives from unionists, peasants, Indigenous people and their allies.

Zé Claudio and Maria's murders were part of this long chain of violence. They lived and worked as nut collectors in the Resex of Praialta Piranheira, in the state of Pará, which they had contributed to creating, and had both been elected leaders of the local occupants' association at various times. They both identified as *caboclos*, a term probably deriving from Amazonian Tupi language that indicates a 'person having copper-coloured skin'[17] or a person of mixed Indigenous Brazilian and European ancestry. *Caboclos* and Indigenous people

---

[17] See https://en.wikipedia.org/wiki/Caboclo

form a large part of the so-called people of the forest. Despite receiving limited formal education, Zé Claudio and Maria had educated themselves politically in the tradition of the rubber tappers movement. Once stablished in Praialta, Maria had gone back to school and pursued a master's in environmental education: she became an educator following the approach of Paulo Freire's pedagogy of the oppressed, and was active in the empowerment of rural women via agroecological projects. Zé Claudio and Maria both believed strongly in agroecology as a socially just and ecologically effective way of preserving the forest, and in the State's obligation to grant Resex communities the exclusive right to own and protect the forest from capitalist encroachment (Milanez, 2015).

Zé Claudio and Maria were not rebels, revolutionaries or forest outlaws: in fact, they believed in the law so strongly to put their lives at risk by denouncing to the authorities the illegal trafficking in timber and the illegal land enclosures that they witnessed in the reserve. Their story, beautifully narrated by Felipe Milanez and Bernardo Loyola in the movie *Toxic: Amazonia* (2011), persuaded the UNEP to award them the Hero of the Forest prize in 2012. Sadly, this recognition has not served to prevent further assassinations, nor to enhance the chances of Praialta Piranheira surviving the current phase of violent dispossessions in the region.

The lives of working-class environmental activists are very seldom celebrated or even recognized as such. The world tends to see them – when they get to be seen – as victims of social injustice, but not as workers who fight and die to save the environment. This lack of understanding, I contend, must be seen as a form of symbolic violence. Denying certain people the right to be recognized as ecological subjects has important material consequences for their lives: it delegitimizes their vision of what the environment is and how it should be preserved, while making them more vulnerable to the master's violence.

Species

Finally, the *Welcome to the Anthropocene* storyline takes anthropocentrism to a new level, that of human geo-supremacy. The Anthropos is redefined as a more-than-species-being: beyond dominating other species, it now rules over the 'forces of Nature' – geological strata and climate. So detached now is the Anthropocene *We* from other living beings, that the living world does not matter to it at all. In representing the geosphere as seen from space, embedded within the abstract lines of an evolving and devouring equation, the video makes the biosphere invisible. Barefacedly adopting the 'God's eye view' of big data, the equation fails to represent the web of life and its sympoietic processes (Haraway, 2016): to man-turned-God, *zoe* does not matter. 'Where is the map showing the overlapping patterns of whale migrations with shipping and military routes?', Stacy Alaimo (2017: 92) asks, noting that, 'The movements, the activities, the liveliness of all creatures' tend to vanish in mainstream representations of the Anthropocene. Nowhere in the video does the narrating voice evoke the principle that humanity's destiny is tied to that of the web of life – a principle that Indigenous cosmogonies have been defending since well before the industrial age (Danowski and Viveiros de Castro, 2017). The objectification of animals that is so essential to industrial farming, fishing and (directly or indirectly) most other aspects of capitalist/industrial modernity, is inexplicably glossed over; the alarming rate of extinction of animal and vegetal species over the last quarter of a century (IPBES, 2019) is only mentioned in passing. What is most emphasized, instead, is human supremacy over the geosphere, symbolizing humanity's rise over the 'forces of nature' – the inanimate physical energies that *Man* has confronted since the beginning of time, and that fossil capitalism has finally overcome via the development of the forces of production.

While coloniality/racism, gender and class are so deeply entrenched in Western culture that they do not require open display as they act through subliminal discursive practices, human geo-supremacy – epitomized by the ability to change climate patterns – is a new feature of the Anthropocene. *We* must be convinced that it holds this power now. However, human supremacy rests upon another key concept of Western modernity, what Teresa Brennan (2000: 8) calls the 'foundational fantasy' of humans imagined as self-contained individuals, justifying the objectification/commodification of other species and of non-human life in general.

Plumwood (1993: 192) attributes human supremacy to the devouring phase of master rationality, in which 'The instrumentalisation of nature takes a totalising form: all planetary life is brought within the sphere of agency of the master (Self).' This foundational fantasy translates into the undisputed right of humanity to rule over non-human nature, and to reshape the physical environment which sustains the web of life in the way that best suits the master's life. Human geo-supremacy takes the objectification of non-human life for granted, and concerns itself exclusively with those non-human, geological forces that are threatening its control over the earth. This distinction between nature as a fragile biodiversity that *We* is losing (a sacrifice to human development) and nature as a strong and autonomous power, a potential enemy to be won over or allied with (Stengers, 2015: 20; see also Merchant, 2016), is another subliminal message that is key to the official Anthropocene story: a twenty-first-century version of the age-old tale of *man vs nature* (Bonneuil and Fressoz, 2017), which now (or perhaps, again) overrides in importance the story of *man vs man*.

Since Carolyn Merchant's (1980) *The death of nature*, ecofeminist thought has pointed to how the European scientific revolution of the seventeenth century turned nature from a living entity (the Renaissance animate cosmos) into a mechanical object, thus allowing the overcoming of (moral) limits to both its knowledge and its exploitation. Capitalist/industrial modernity would be unthinkable without that fundamental shift in consciousness. In *Ecological revolutions*, Merchant (1989) also documented the colonial extension of the *death of nature*. She showed how, in colonial New England, Native American understandings of home as place (*oikos*), that is, the natural habitat, in a non-ownership relationship of 'face-to-face material subjects in a space-time web' was replaced by the patriarchal conception of home as a secluded space for human reproduction through domestication of plant and animal life, based on unpaid and/or slave labour (the master's house), and aimed at turning non-human life into 'objects of extraction' (Merchant, 1989: 67–8).

More recently, Anna Tsing (2012) has made similar observations regarding the history of fungi as related to the colonial extension of the patriarchal family, private property and the modern State. Overall, ecofeminist thought extends the concept of intersectionality beyond the human, that is, it explores the intersected violence that oppresses living beings along lines of both social and species inequalities (Bird Rose, 2013; Gaard, 1993, 2011). In being subject to different forms of oppression within a common matrix – colonial/capitalist/heteropatriarchy – these subjects are seen as a more-than-human community of kindred beings (Gaard, 1997; Mortimer-Sandilands and Erickson, 2010).

Not only has ecofeminist thought questioned the hyper-separation between human and non-human life, but also similar dualisms of mind/body and subject/object. Inspired by Indigenous knowledge as well as by a number of Western 'traitor scientists' (Stengers, 2015) – evolutionary biologists, ethologists and quantum physicists – ecofeminists have come to claim that 'evidence across many life forms including plants is increasingly indicating the widespread, possibly universal, existence of sentience and agency' (Bird Rose, 2013: 97). In her book *Ecological culture*, Plumwood (2002: 176) argued for the importance of adopting a post-cartesian rationality that would enable us to recognize 'earth others as fellow agents and narrative subjects' within a 'dialogical conception of self' – a step towards enhancing 'interspecies communication'. According to Deborah Bird Rose, Plumwood's philosophical animism is a call for negotiating 'life membership of an ecological community of kindred beings' (Plumwood, 2009, quoted in Bird Rose, 2013: 98).

Over the past decade, material feminism and feminist science and technology studies have greatly contributed to an exploration of transcorporeal affections, that is, the entanglements of human with non-human life within a common material reality that characterize the Anthropocene (Alaimo, 2017; Alaimo and Hekman, 2008). The history of this epoch could now be re-written as one of collective and interspecies 'toxic (auto)biographies' (Armiero et al., 2019) made up of the countless stories – like those of sheep/dioxin/human entanglements in Acerra, Italy (Armiero and Fava, 2016) – that testify to the uneven patterns through which environmental injustice has been inscribed in the planet's 'organosphere'.[18]

Interspecies entanglements and cosmopolitical interaction do not only speak of the 'slow violence' (Nixon, 2011) of capitalist/industrial modernity; they also, and perhaps more importantly, tell stories of anti-extractive and anti-capitalist resistance, of life's counteraction to metabolic rifts (Tola, 2019). Acknowledging these stories leads one to wonder about the possibility of rethinking Marx's concept of species-being towards conceptualizing an *inter-species-being*, that is, a being-with and becoming-with of humans and non-humans that may enact a new 'dignified mode of humanity' (Roelvink, 2013) and co-constitute new political subjects in the form of 'cross-species alliances of bios and zoe' (Braidotti, 2017). This alternate approach to the meaning of humanity, as Serenella Iovino (2019) reminds us, would acknowledge and rediscover the common roots between the *human* and *humus* – the soil – via an attitude of *humility* (rather than supremacy).

These interrogations of ecofeminism, material feminism and decolonial thought intersect in Donna Haraway's *Staying with the trouble*, which reminds us that 'No species, not even our own arrogant one pretending to be good individuals in so-called modern Western scripts, acts alone; assemblages of organic species and of abiotic actors make history, the evolutionary kind and the other kinds too' (Haraway, 2016: 100). She proposes that, with its dramatic reconfigurations of the web of life, the Anthropocene should be seen as a time of passage towards something new, an epoch of 'multispecies ecojustice'. For this to happen, Haraway argues, it is necessary to invest our collective energies in a 'recomposition of kin' which might be allowed 'by the fact that all earthlings are kin in the deepest sense, and it is past time to practice better care of kinds-assemblages (not species one at a time)' (Haraway, 2016: 103).

Undoing the hyper-separations that have allowed for human geo-supremacy is a political project, in the sense that it would create the possibility for a different, non-master mode of humanity to be acknowledged and struggled for. Different kinds of institutions – be they labs and research centres, schools, museums, governance agencies or community organizations – are inevitably involved in this kind of project. Permaculture practices, for example, challenge

---

[18] See the multimedia map of the Toxic Bios project: www.toxicbios.eu

both standardized systems of capitalist valuation and socially conservative understandings of place. Reflecting on the Italian network *Genuino Clandestino*, for example, Laura Centemeri (2018: 299) has proposed that permaculture should be understood as 'multispecies commoning', that is, a praxis of satisfying subsistence needs by activating communities of response that 'consciously involve a variety of beings and entities' towards a reconfiguration of value practices. What permaculture theorists and movements have rediscovered, it could be argued, are those agro/forestry practices of peasant and Indigenous communities that may have managed to keep themselves at least partly free from colonial/capitalist relations – or are struggling to do so.

This is certainly the case in the experience of Praialta Piranheira, the home of Zé Claudio and Maria, where people had come together to reclaim the possibility for themselves to re/exist *with* the forest – as Maria used to say – that is, to reconfigure their livelihood and political existence as members of a forest community (*forestzenship*), rather than outside it. When he first met the Brazilian reporter Felipe Milanez, in October 2010, Zé Claudio took him to see Majestade, the secular Brazil-nut tree (*castanheira*) that stood at the centre of the land plot that he and Maria had made their home. He could not possibly tell Felipe his own story without also telling him about *hers*.[19] The very first scenes of the movie *Toxic: Amazonia* show Zé Claudio walking through a shady, lush vegetation, then stopping before a large trunk, his arm reaching out to it and his palm delicately touching the bark. 'This is Majestade, the pride of the forest', he announces, showing Felipe the width and height of the plant. 'If it was for me', he adds, 'she would remain here for many years still.' He pauses, both his arms reaching out to the tree, both his palms touching the green stratum covering the bark: 'Even if she died, if something happened to her, this trunk will still be here', he says, before lowering his head and turning to look away.

When the PAE (agro-forestry project) of Praialta Piranheira was created back in 1997, Zé Claudio recounted, 85 per cent of the area was covered by native forest stands, mainly *castanha* (*Bertholletia excelsa*) and *cupuaçu* (*Theobroma grandiflorum*); little more than 20 per cent of it had survived by 2010, he claimed, parcelled in different places and surrounded by monocrop plantations. 'It's a disaster for those like me, the *extrativistas*', he commented. A Brazil-nut collector since the age of seven, Zé Claudio self-identified with the *castanheira* and could not imagine his life without it: 'I live of the forest, and I protect her by all means', he claimed. Maria, who had also grown up with *castanha*, shared the

---

[19] The Portuguese word *castanha*, as well as *castanheira* (Brazil-nut tree), *árvore* (tree) and *floresta* (forest) are all feminine

same life project. She made it clear that it was a contested project, one that required political struggle and might imply losing one's life. 'Until there is a *castanheira* here, I am willing to fight. Until there is one, I'll give my blood for her', she declared (Milanez, 2015: 63–4). Zé Claudio and Maria saw no hyper-separation between their lives and that of their home forest: the *castanheira* was their companion species, and the *castanhal* (castanheira forest) the more-than-human commons of which they were kindred members.

The Praialta story suggests the possibility of developing a historical-materialist approach to interspecies-being, seeing it as an insurgent practice of contesting the hyper-separation predicated by colonial/capitalist/heteropatriar-chal modernity; that is, as an alternate mode of social emancipation and full realization of human potential. While Marx intended species-being as a means to a dignified way of living through the affirmation of distinctive human potentialities – that is, the sensuous appropriation of non-human nature – interspecies-being could be understood as a recognition of the active role played by non-human nature in the realization of human potential. As Gerda Roelvink (2013) explains, 'appropriation in species-being refers to the interdependence of the human species with "earth others" as they become part of, transform (and are transformed by), and thereby constitute humanity.' Inter-species being, I suggest, could take full account of this co-constitution of humans with earth others as realized through a more-than-human labour process.

Here it becomes useful to employ Alyssa Battistoni's (2017: 5) concept of hybrid labour, which she defines as a 'collective, distributed undertaking of humans and nonhumans acting to reproduce, regenerate, and renew a common world'. As she puts it:

> Hybrid labor helps thread the needle between anthropocentrically instrumen-tal and purely intrinsic value, recognizing the useful, material productivity of nonhuman nature without reducing it to the status of object or tool. . . . it aims to call a more-than-human political collective into being, and to propose a relationship to nonhuman nature grounded in interdependence and solidar-ity rather than unidirectional management, ownership, or stewardship. (Battistoni, 2017: 6)

The relevance of hybrid labour to the Praialta story consists in making visible how this life project was radically alternative to the *valorization* of non-human life as realized in old and new forms of capitalist/industrial modernity. It does so by allowing the conceptualization of labour's potentialities for different ways of preserving and of valuing non-human nature. Praialta itself could be seen as a result of hybrid labour: as ethnobotanical research has shown, before Zé Claudio and Maria went to live there, the *castanhal* had formed out of a process of inter-species becoming. Its geographical concentration in the South of Pará was related to the nomadic Indigenous habitations of this area, with their intensive use of the fruit as a source of protein (Milanez, 2015). The agro-extractivist life project consisted in both appropriating *and* reproducing this inter-species assemblage (the *castanhal*) by making a living within it.

This project, however, required the expenditure not only of hybrid labour but of political engagement and active citizenship (*forestzenship*, more appropriately). With the advancement of colonial/capitalist modernity in the twentieth century, the *castanhal* had become a disputed forest, its r/existence depending on social struggles opposing developmental plans based on the expansion of iron mining and other commodities. The region of Tocantins-Araguaia – where the PAE of Praialta was located – had a long history of violence against both the *castanhal* and its people – Gaviões, Aikewara, Xikrin, Parakana, Assurini, Kayapó, caboclos, peasants, *nut collectors* – a history of which Zé Claudio and Maria were active subjects (Milanez, 2015). Clearly, they feared that violence could happen to Praialta, to Majestade and to them. Maria's sister Laísa also lived in the PAE with her family and animals: her house, where she was interviewed by Felipe Milanez and Bernardo Loyola, was a simple shack surrounded by vegetation, with an annexed workshop. 'This is our home', she says, smiling, 'our paradise, where we live.' Laísa and her husband Rondon then take the two visitors to see the plot, showing them the plants that grow there – cocoa, *cupuaçu*, *castanha* – and they stop by a slim, smooth trunk. 'This is the Amazon's gold, mahogany', Laísa says proudly. After the assassination, they had to leave their home for a while; they were scared that something could happen to the family. But fear could not prevail, and they returned to their paradise after a few months. 'I would not trade it with anything, I really wouldn't', Laísa adds.

Castanhas and *nut collectors* were members of a forest community born out of both hybrid labour and political struggle, whose permanence was threatened by the advancement of capitalist/industrial modernity. This is not a pristine wilderness to preserve, but a *naturcultural* terrain where the metabolic rift of the Anthropocene is contested and opposed by Indigenous and peasant populations that configure as forces of reproduction. Humans defend the *castanhal* because this is the nature they have materially *appropriated* through long-standing metabolic interactions, making it fit for their subsistence. It is this inter-species being, it could be argued, that attracts hatred and disavowal on the part of those subjects that identify with the capitalist project, which presupposes the *death of nature* and its objectification into a passive, mechanical means to the production of value. To Zé Claudio, Maria and Laísa, the *castanhal* is a living entity whose existence is not easily distinguishable from their own: it is this obstinate refusal of objectification that make them seen as enemies of progress.

In this sense, Laísa's definition of the *castanhal* as *nosso paraíso* ('our paradise') evokes the contested but nonetheless real existence of a counter-capitalist world, in which people become free from exploitation and alienation *together with* rather than *away from* non-human nature. Liberation here assumes a more-than-human meaning: there can be no true emancipation in a degraded and threatened environment where earth-others are sacrificed. As their interviews (Milanez, 2015) suggest, the commoners of Praialta are well aware that, while monocultures may be rich in market *value* (at least for a number of years), they are poor in common-*wealth* – diversity, freedom, resilience, beauty, community, happiness. As a result of inter-species becoming (of hybrid labour and political struggle, of more-than-human life and death), the *castanhal* is worth incommensurably more than any commodity. Inexplicable as it may seem, there are people who orientate their lives around this different kind of value. This, I would argue, is an alternate mode of humanity that is at once desperately needed and yet utterly absent from the hegemonic Anthropocene narrative.

Conclusions

The thesis put forth in this Element is that undoing the Anthropocene and making space for counter-hegemonic modes of habitation of the earth requires seeing and valuing the forces of reproduction. This, I have argued, does not imply an exclusive focus on women's agency as earthcarers, but rather a radical rejection of the gender/colonial/species/class relations embedded in the master model of modernity. Although ecofeminism was born and still is a predominantly women's movement, you don't need to be a woman to share its vision and praxis (nor do all women embrace it either). The multitude of collectives that struggle to defend the principles of commoning, eco-sufficiency and global environmental justice in different parts of the world cannot be identified as women's movements. Even though empirical research has shown that women are predominantly active in these reproduction/justice-oriented collectives – rather than in eco-modernist, governmental or green growth initiatives – it would be wrong to conclude that it is in their nature to do so.

Moreover, this would obviously legitimize the sexual division of labour that sits at the very core of the ecological crisis. In feminist political ecology the point is not to romanticize women's engagement with grassroots eco/peace activism, but to show how this is the result of sexual divisions of labour from the local to the global scale. The aim is that of abolishing heteropatriarchy, thus liberating people from gender roles – particularly, those of man the money-maker-who-destroys-nature and woman the life-maker-who-saves-nature. Ecofeminists see this as a preliminary step towards (rather than a consequence of) combating the racial/ colonial division of labour, class inequalities and speciesism – the other ways through which capital devalues labour, putting profit above lives. Coloniality, gender, class and species all matter to the Anthropocene: the struggles to undo each of them are intersected with each other and cannot be separated. Together, they form the essence of what the climate justice movement calls 'system change'.

This political vision requires a rethinking of historical materialism in eco-feminist terms. The process of global proletarianization that has accompanied the Anthropocene generated not only ecological but also social and political contradictions; it served to keep wage-labour divided from the unwaged and from non-human nature. By focussing on industrial wage-labour, Marxist theory and labour organizations have often missed this strategic contradiction, maintaining a problematic separation between labour, feminist, Indigenous, peasant and environmental struggles – or, between the interests and struggles of industrial and meta-industrial workers. An ecofeminist perspective suggests that the crux of the matter for a truly radical political ecology consists in broadening the semantic sphere of labour towards the inclusion of both industrial and meta-industrial work in their dialectical historical relationship. This would allow broadening the scope of labour environmentalism, enhancing its potentialities as an agent of ecological revolution.

Historical materialism – the theory of class struggle as the fundamental driver of change – would be expanded beyond the exclusive realm of a conflict between capitalists and wage-earners who resist exploitation and the depletion of bodies, to include all those subjects of earthcare that resist value extraction and the degradation of earth-systems. Such a renewed vision of historical materialism would allow thinking in terms of alliances between industrial and meta-industrial workers based on a common material interest in keeping the world alive by transforming the relations of re/production. Such alliances must involve those sciences and technologies which are appropriate to, or already mobilized in, counter-master projects of earthcare. In other words, undoing the Anthropocene and building new ecological relations requires a radical politicization of science and technology, that is, their mobilization as counter-master tools.

This approach differs substantially from eco-modernist calls to fully embrace the forces of production, in the sense of taking collective responsibility for the unintended consequences of industrial modernity, and embarking on an even higher level of mastering earth-systems.[20] Such an approach, I contend, represents an industrial/masculinist version of care. Like the *Welcome to the*

---

[20] See for example: http://www.ecomodernism.org/

Anthropocene storyline, it reflects the privileged point of view of those who have made the Anthropocene their home, rather than those who have suffered and resisted it; it postulates a master subject who takes care of inferior others that depend on it – rather than vice-versa. Moreover, it assumes the master model of modernity as universal, discounting as irrelevant the class/gender/species/racial oppressions that it has embedded. All this derives from assuming a hegemonic, post-political understanding of the forces of production as master's tools, and ignoring/silencing the non-master subjectivities that have also made modernity, and their alternate praxes of earthcare.

My vision for a post-Anthropocene world, on the contrary, starts from acknowledging that life in the Anthropocene is the result of a painful history of counter-mastering. It implies acknowledging the truly earthcaring possibilities that can be opened up by liberating the forces of re/production. The counter-plantation (slave plot), Indigenous conservation projects, subsistence provisioning, women's reproductive autonomy, factory occupations, unions' environmental struggles, community gardening and reforestation projects, agroecology, permaculture and extractive reserves, I have argued, represent non-master ways of countering metabolic rift, aimed at re-commoning the means of re/production. This is not a comprehensive list, of course; many more instances could be added, other stories excavated from the oblivion of the master's narrative. Brought together, these alternate Anthropocene subjects and their praxes could turn earthcare into a new, truly emancipatory ecological revolution.

Epilogue: Within and beyond the COVID-19 Pandemic

While this Element was under review for publication, in February–March 2020, the COVID-19 pandemic struck, demonstrating with painful clarity the validity of ecofeminist critiques of industrial modernity. The mastering of non-human life has been the fundamental cause of the inter-species spread of the SARS-CoV-2 virus, but the master's denial of inter-species dependencies has been firmly tied with its backgrounding of the forces of reproduction. Centuries of colonialism, sexism and class war have pushed women and subsistence producers like Zé Claudio and Maria off the land to make space for industrial farming and other forms of plundering, with destructive effects on wildlife habitats and food production. As a consequence, the world now faces an unprecedented threat to human health, but it does so unequally.

Governmental responses, demanding the sacrifice of health care workers (together with that of other workers deemed essential to national fiscal balance), have demonstrated, once again, that capitalism is structured to put profit above life. After decades of neoliberal cuts to welfare and health care provision worldwide, women, refugees, disabled people and other vulnerable groups are facing an unprecedented increase in the burden of care; women and transgender people are also facing death and increasing threats that come not from the virus itself but from domestic violence, homelessness or discrimination in access to care. Precarious workers, peasants and poor people have undergone the loss of their livelihoods, and the spectre of hunger is looming over the world. The Indigenous and extractivist populations of Amazonia are facing genocide.

Ecofeminist politics has become more important than ever; this recognition is now making possible the alliance of different movements representing the forces of reproduction. One way in which this alliance is taking shape is through the demand for a care income, promoted by the Global Women's Strike and Women of Colour GWS movements.[21] Representing a convergence of 'wages for housework' with degrowth and climate justice perspectives, the care income demand recognizes the crucial value of care work as a means for radical change in global political economy. It urges governments to 'invest in caring, not killing', by dropping financial support for fossil fuels, the arms trade and industrial farming and diverting money towards supporting caregivers in homes and communities, as well as in urban and rural environments.

A care income would recognize the work of people like Zé Claudio and Maria as truly essential to keeping the world alive; it would give agroecology projects such as Praialta Piranheira the possibility of thriving and multiplying, halting global metabolic rift, putting healthy food on the tables of poor people and preventing new pandemics in the future. This is not an all-encompassing plan for undoing the Anthropocene with one coup, but it would certainly help in dismantling the master's house.

---

[21] The care income demand originated as part of the Green New Deal for Europe campaign (https://gndforeurope.com), through a joint effort by Selma James, Nina López, Giacomo D'Alisa and myself. It then spread beyond Europe through an international mobilization that reached a number of countries, including the USA, where it was endorsed by the Poor People Campaign at its digital march on Washington in June 2020. See Open letter to governments: a care income now!: https://docs.google.com/forms/d/e/1FAIpQLSfJS_qM-zyku4ig2YajtyO1BLOSTu4da0u7__BlQup-7fGIhw/viewform

References

Acemoglu, D. (2009). *Introduction to modern economic growth*, Princeton, NJ: Princeton University Press.

Acker, J. (2006). *Class questions: feminist answers*, Lanham, MD: Rowman & Littlefield.

Adamson, J., Gleason, W. A. and Pellow, D. N. (eds.). (2016). *Keywords for environmental studies*, New York, NY: New York University Press.

Agamben, G. (1995). *Homo sacer: il potere sovrano e la nuda vita*, Turin: Giulio Einaudi.

Agyeman, J. (2014). Global environmental justice or le droit au monde? *Geoforum*, **54**, 236–8. http://doi.org/10.1016/j.geoforum.2012.12.021

Agyeman, J. and Ogneva-Himmelberger, Y. (2009). *Environmental justice and sustainability in the former Soviet Union*, Cambridge, MA: MIT Press.

Alaimo, S. (2010). *Bodily natures: science, environment, and the material self*, Bloomington, IN: Indiana University Press.

Alaimo, S. (2017). Your shell on acid: material immersion, Anthropocene dissolves. In R. Grusin, ed., *Anthropocene feminism*, Minneapolis, MN: University of Minnesota Press, pp. 89–120.

Alaimo, S. and Hekman, S. J. (eds.). (2008). *Material feminisms*, Bloomington, IN: Indiana University Press.

Apostolopoulou, E. and Cortes-Vazquez, J. A. (2018). *The right to nature: social movements, environmental justice and neoliberal natures*, London: Routledge.

Armiero, M. and De Angelis, M. (2017). Anthropocene: victims, narrators, and revolutionaries. *South Atlantic Quarterly*, **116**(2), 345–62. http://doi.org/10.1215/00382876-3829445

Armiero, M. and Fava, A. (2016). Of humans, sheep, and dioxin: a history of contamination and transformation in Acerra, Italy. *Capitalism Nature Socialism*, **27**(2), 67–82. http://doi.org/10.1080/10455752.2016.1172812

Armiero, M. and Tucker, R. (2017). *Environmental history of modern migrations*, London: Routledge.

Armiero, M., Andritsos, T. and Barca, S. et al. (2019). Toxic Bios: toxic autobiographies – a public environmental humanities project. *Environmental Justice*, **12**(1), 7–11. http://doi.org/10.1089/env.2018.0019

Arruzza, C., Bhattacharya, T., and Fraser, N. (2019). *Feminism for the 99 percent: a manifesto*, London: Verso.

Asher, K. (2017). Spivak and Rivera Cusicanqui on the dilemmas of representation in postcolonial and decolonial feminisms. *Feminist Studies*, **43**(3), 512–24. http://doi.org/10.15767/feministstudies.43.3.0512

Balée, W. L. (1994). *Footprints of the forest: Ka'apor ethnobotany – the historical ecology of plant utilization by an Amazonian people*, New York, NY: Columbia University Press.

Barbosa de Almeida, M. (2008). A enciclopédia da floresta e a florestania. https://mwba.files.wordpress.com/2010/06/2008-almeida-a-florestania-e-a-enciclopedia-da-floresta-texto.pdf

Barca, S. (2010). *Enclosing water: nature and political economy in a Mediterranean valley, 1796–1916*, Cambridge, UK: White Horse Press.

Barca, S. (2011). Energy, property and the industrial revolution narrative. *Ecological Economics*, **70**(7), 1309–15.

Barca, S. and Bridge, G. (2015). Industrialization and environmental change. In T. Perreault, G. Bridge and J. McCarthy, eds., *The Routledge handbook of political ecology*, London: Routledge, pp. 366–77.

Barca, S. and Leonardi, E. (2018). Working-class ecology and union politics: a conceptual topology. *Globalizations*, **15**(4), 487–503. http://doi.org/10.1080/14747731.2018.1454672

Barca, S., Chertkovskaya, E. and Paulsson, A. (2019). The end of political economy as we knew it? From growth realism to nomadic utopianism. In E. Chertkovskaya, A. Paulsson and S. Barca, eds., *Towards a political economy of degrowth*, London: Rowman & Littlefield International, pp. 1–18.

Barca, S. and Milanez, F. (in press). Labouring the commons. Amazonia's extractive reserves and the legacy of Chico Mendes. In N. Räthzel, D. Stevis and D. Uzzell, eds., *Handbook of environmental labour studies,*. London: Palgrave

Barlow, J., Parry, L., Gardner, T. A., Lees, A. C. and Peres, C. A. (2012). Developing evidence-based arguments to assess the pristine nature of Amazonian forests. *Biological Conservation*, **152**, 293–4. http://doi.org/10.1016/j.biocon.2012.03.024

Batthacharya, T. (2017). *Social reproduction theory: remapping class, recentering oppression*, London: Pluto Press.

Batthacharya, T. (2019). Three ways a green new deal can promote life over capital. *Jacobin*, 6 October. https://jacobinmag.com/2019/06/green-new-deal-social-care-work

Battistoni, A. (2017). Bringing in the work of nature: from natural capital to hybrid labor. *Political Theory*, **45**(1), 5–31. http://doi.org/10.1177/0090591716638389

Bauhardt, C. (2019). Nature, care and gender: feminist dilemmas. In C. Bauhardt and W. Harcourt, eds., *Feminist political ecology and the economics of care: in search of economic alternatives*, London: Routledge, pp. 16–35.

Bauhardt, C. and Harcourt, W. (eds.). (2019). *Feminist political ecology and the economics of care: in search of economic alternatives*, London: Routledge.

Bell, S. E. (2013). *Our roots run deep as ironweed: Appalachian women and the fight for environmental justice*, Urbana, IL: University of Illinois Press.

Bhambra, G. K. (2007). *Rethinking modernity: postcolonialism and the sociological imagination*, London: Palgrave.

Biesecker, A. and Hofmeister, S. (2010). Focus: (re)productivity: sustainable relations both between society and nature and between the genders. *Ecological Economics*, **69**(8), 1703–11. http://doi.org/10.1016/j.ecolecon.2010.03.025

Bird Rose, D. (2013). Val Plumwood's philosophical animism: attentive interactions in the sentient world. *Environmental humanities*, **3**(1), 93–109. http://doi.org/10.1215/22011919-3611248

Bond, P. (2019). Degrowth, devaluation and uneven development from North to South. In E. Chertkovskaya, A. Paulsson and S. Barca, eds., *Towards a political economy of degrowth*, London: Rowman & Littlefield International, pp. 137–56.

Bonneuil, C. and Fressoz, J.-B. (2017). *The shock of the Anthropocene: the earth, history and us*, London: Verso.

Braidotti, R. (2017). Four theses on posthuman feminism. In R. Grusin, ed., *Anthropocene feminism*, Minneapolis, MN: University of Minnesota Press.

Brand, U. and Wissen, M. (2013). Crisis and continuity of capitalist society–nature relationships: the imperial mode of living and the limits to environmental governance. *Review of International Political Economy*, **20**(4), 687–711. http://doi.org/10.1080/09692290.2012.691077

Bravo, E., and Moreano, M. (2015). Whose good living? Post neo-liberalism, the green state and subverted alternatives to development in Ecuador. In R. L. Bryant, ed., *The international handbook of political ecology*, Cheltenham, UK: Edward Elgar Publishing, pp. 332–44.

Brennan, T. (2000). *Exhausting modernity: grounds for a new economy*, London: Routledge.

Brennan, T. (2003). *Globalization and its terrors: daily life in the West*, London: Routledge.

Brown, K. (2017). Global environmental change II: planetary boundaries – a safe operating space for human geographers? *Progress in Human Geography*, **41**(1), 118–30. http://doi.org/10.1177/0309132515604429

Brugnaro, F. (1997). *Fist of sun*, Evanston, IL: Curbstone Press.

Bryant, R. L. (ed.). (2015). *The international handbook of political ecology*, Cheltenham, UK: Edward Elgar Publishing.

Buckingham-Hatfield, S. (2000). *Gender and environment*, London: Routledge.

Bullard, R. D. (2000). *Dumping in Dixie: race, class, and environmental quality*, 3rd edition, London: Routledge.

Burgmann, M. and Burgmann, V. (1998). *Green bans, red union: environmental activism and the New South Wales builders labourers' federation*, Sydney: University of New South Wales Press.

Butler, J. (1990). *Gender trouble: feminism and the subversion of identity*, New York, NY: Routledge.

Butler, J. (2004). *Undoing gender*, New York, NY: Routledge.

Cabnal, L. (2010). Acercamiento a la construcción del pensamiento epistémico de las mujeres indígenas feministas comunitarias de Abya Yala. In ACSUR, ed., *Feminismos diversos: el feminismo comunitario*, Madrid: ACSUR – Las Segovias, pp. 10–25.

Caffentzis, G. and Federici, S. (2014). Commons against and beyond capitalism. *Community Development Journal*, **49**(suppl 1), i92–i105. http://doi.org/10.1093/cdj/bsu006

Casimir, J. (2010). Reckoning in Haiti. http://forums.ssrc.org/haiti/author/jean-casimir/

Casselot, M. A. (2016). Ecofeminist echoes in new materialism? *PhænEx*, **11**(1), 73–96.

Centemeri, L. (2018). Commons and the new environmentalism of everyday life. Alternative value practices and multispecies commoning in the permaculture movement. *Rassegna Italiana Di Sociologia*, **59**(2), 289–314. http://doi.org/10.1423/90581

Charkiewicz, E. (2009). Who is the 'He' of he who decides in economic discourse? In A. Salleh, ed., *Eco-sufficiency and global justice: women write political ecology*, London: Pluto Press, pp. 66–86.

Chertkovskaya, E. (2019). Degrowth in theory, pursuit of growth in action: exploring the Russian and Soviet contexts. In E. Chertkovskaya, A. Paulsson and S. Barca, eds., *Towards a political economy of degrowth*, London: Rowman & Littlefield International, pp. 101–20.

Chirico, R. (2015). *Plastica: storia di Donato Chirico, operaio petrolchimico*, Calimera, Italy: Kurumuny.

Cielemęcka, O. and Åsberg, C. (2019). Introduction: toxic embodiment and feminist environmental humanities. *Environmental Humanities*, **11**(1), 101–7. http://doi.org/10.1215/22011919-7349433

Clark, B. and Foster, J. B. (2009). Ecological imperialism and the global metabolic rift: unequal exchange and the guano/nitrates trade. *International Journal of Comparative Sociology*, **50**(3–4), 311–34. http://doi.org/10.1177/0020715209105144

Clark, B. and York, R. (2005). Carbon metabolism: global capitalism, climate change, and the biospheric rift. *Theory and Society*, 34(4), 391–428. http://doi.org/10.1007/s11186-005-1993-4

Clark, G. (2007). *A farewell to alms: a brief economic history of the world*, Princeton, NJ: Princeton University Press.

Cohn, S. (ed.). (2015). *Ailton Krenak*, Rio de Janeiro: Azougue.

Colectivo Miradas Críticas del Territorio desde el Feminismo. (2017). Mapeando el cuerpo-territorio. Guía metodológica para mujeres que defienden sus territories. https://territorioyfeminismos.org/2017/11/13/guia-mapeando-el-cuerpo-territorio/

Connell, R. W. (1985). Theorising gender. *Sociology*, **19**(2), 260–72. http://doi.org/10.1177/0038038585019002008

Dalla Costa, M. (2003). The native in us, the earth we belong to. *The Commoner*, **6**, 1–34.

Danowski, D. and Viveiros de Castro, E. (2017). *The ends of the world*, Cambridge: Polity Press.

Davis, M. (2017). *Planet of slums*, London: Verso.

Davis, H. and Todd, Z. (2017). On the importance of a date, or decolonizing the Anthropocene. *ACME: An International Journal for Critical Geographies*, **16**(4), 761–80.

Davis, J., Moulton, A. A., Van Sant, L. and Williams, B. (2019). Anthropocene, Capitalocene, . . . Plantationocene?: a manifesto for ecological justice in an age of global crises. *Geography Compass*, **13**(5), e12438. http://doi.org/10.1111/gec3.12438

De Angelis, M. (2017). *Omnia sunt communia: on the commons and the transformation to postcapitalism*, London: Zed Books.

De Ishtar, Z. (2009). Nuclearised bodies and militarised space. In A. Salleh, ed., *Eco-sufficiency and global justice: women write political ecology*, London: Pluto Press, pp. 121–39.

Death, C. (2010). *Governing sustainable development: partnerships, protests and power at the world summit*, London: Routledge.

Di Chiro, G. (2017). Welcome to the white (M)anthropocene? In S. MacGregor, ed., *Routledge handbook of gender and environment*, London: Routledge, pp. 487–505.

Dombroski, K., Healy, S. and McKinnon, K. (2019). Care-full community economies. In C. Bauhardt and W. Harcourt, eds., *Feminist political ecology and the economics of care: in search of economic alternatives*, 1st edition, Abingdon, UK and New York: Routledge, pp. 99–115.

Dussel, E. (1993). Eurocentrism and modernity (introduction to the Frankfurt Lectures). *Boundary 2*, **20**(3), 65–76. http://doi.org/10.2307/303341

Escobar, A. (2008). *Territories of difference: place, movements, life, redes*, Durham, NC: Duke University Press.

Espinosa, Y., Gómez, D. and Ochoa, K. (eds.). (2014). *Tejiendo de outro modo: feminismo, epistemología y apuestas descoloniales en Abya Yala*, Popayán: Editorial Universidad del Cauca.

Fakier, K. and Cock, J. (2018). Eco-feminist organizing in South Africa: reflections on the feminist table. *Capitalism Nature Socialism*, **29**(1), 40–57. http://doi.org/10.1080/10455752.2017.1421980

Federici, S. (2004). *Caliban and the witch*, Brooklyn, NY: Autonomedia.

Federici, S. (2009). The devaluation of women's labour. In A. Salleh, ed., *Eco-sufficiency and global justice: women write political ecology*, London: Pluto Press, pp.43–65.

Federici, S. (2010). Feminism and the politics of the commons in an era of primitive accumulation. In C. Hughes, S. Peace and K. V. Meter, eds., *Uses of a whirlwind: movement, movements, and contemporary radical currents in the United States*, Oakland, CA: AK Press, pp. 283–94.

Ferguson, S. (2019). *Women and work feminism, labour, and social reproduction*, London: Pluto Press.

Fisher, M. (2009). *Capitalist realism: is there no alternative?*, Winchester, UK: Zero Books.

Foster, J. B. (2000). *Marx's ecology: materialism and nature*, New York, NY: New York University Press.

Fraser, N. (2014). Behind Marx's hidden abode. *New Left Review*, **86**, 55–72.

Gaard, G. (1993). Living interconnections with animals and nature. In G. Gaard, ed., *Ecofeminism: women, animals, nature*, Philadelphia, PA: Temple University Press, pp. 1–12.

Gaard, G. (1997). Toward a queer ecofeminism. *Hypatia*, **12**(1), 114–37. http://doi.org/10.1111/j.1527-2001.1997.tb00174.x

Gaard, G. (2011). Ecofeminism revisited: rejecting essentialism and re-placing species in a material feminist environmentalism. *Feminist Formations*, **23**(2), 26–53.

Gaard, G. (2015). Ecofeminism and climate change. *Women's Studies International Forum*, **49**, 20–33. http://doi.org/10.1016/j.wsif.2015.02.004

Giacomini, T. (2018). The 2017 United Nations climate summit: women fighting for system change and building the commons at COP23 in Bonn, Germany. *Capitalism Nature Socialism*, **29**(1), 89–105. http://doi.org/10.1080/10455752.2018.1434217

Gibson-Graham, J.-K, Resnick, S. R. and Wolff, R. D. (eds.). (2000). *Class and its others*, Minneapolis, MN: University of Minnesota Press.

Global Witness. (2017). Defenders of the earth: global killings of land and environmental defenders in 2016. https://www.globalwitness.org/sv/campaigns/environmental-activists/defenders-earth/

Goodman, J. and Salleh, A. (2013). The 'green economy': class hegemony and counter-hegemony. *Globalizations*, **10**(3), 411–24. http://doi.org/10.1080/14747731.2013.787770

Gowdy, J., and O'Hara, S. (1997). Weak sustainability and viable technologies. *Ecological Economics*, **22**(3), 239–47. http://doi.org/10.1016/S0921-8009(97)00093-1

Gregoratti, C. and Raphael, R. (2019). The historical roots of a feminist 'degrowth': Maria Mies and Marilyn Waring's critiques of growth. In E. Chertkovskaya, A. Paulsson and S. Barca, eds., *Towards a political economy of degrowth*, London: Rowman & Littlefield International, pp. 83–98.

Guillamón, À. and Ruiz, C. (2015). Feminismos y lucha por el territorio en América Latina. *Pueblos*, **64**. http://www.revistapueblos.org/blog/2015/02/09/feminismos-y-lucha-por-el-territorio-en-america-latina/

Guillaumin, C. (1995). *Racism, sexism, power and ideology*, London: Routledge.

Hall, S. (1992). The West and the rest: discourse and power. In S. Hall and B. Gieben, eds., *Formations of modernity*, Oxford: Polity Press, pp. 184–227.

Hamilton, C. (2015). Human destiny in the Anthropocene. In C. Hamilton, F. Gemenne and C. Bonneuil, eds., *The Anthropocene and the global environmental crisis: rethinking modernity in a new epoch*, New York, NY: Routledge, pp. 32–43.

Haraway, D. (1991). *Simians, cyborgs, and women: the reinvention of nature*, New York, NY: Routledge.

Haraway, D. J. (2016). *Staying with the trouble: making kin in the Chthulucene*, Durham, NC: Duke University Press.

Harcourt, W. and Bauhardt, C. (2019). Introduction: conversations on care in feminist political economy and ecology. In C. Bauhardt and W. Harcourt, eds., *Feminist political ecology and the economics of care: in search of economic alternatives*, London: Routledge, pp. 1–15.

Harcourt, W. and Nelson, I. L. (2015). *Practising feminist political ecologies: moving beyond the 'green economy'*, London: Zed Books.

Harvey, D. (1999). The environment of justice. In F. Fischer and M. A. Hajer, eds., *Living with nature: environmental politics as cultural discourse*, Oxford: Oxford University Press.

Harvey, D. (2003). *The new imperialism*, Oxford: Oxford University Press.

Healy, H., Martínez-Alier, J. and Kallis, G. (2015). From ecological modernization to socially sustainable economic degrowth: lessons from ecological economics. In R. L. Bryant, ed., *The international handbook of political ecology*, Cheltenham, UK: Edward Elgar Publishing, pp. 577–90.

Hecht, S. B. and Cockburn, A. (2010). *The fate of the forest: developers, destroyers, and defenders of the Amazon*, Chicago, IL: University of Chicago Press.

Hickel, J., and Kallis, G. (2020). Is green growth possible? *New Political Economy*, 25(4), 469–86. https://doi.org/10.1080/13563467.2019.1598964

Houston, D. (2013). Environmental justice storytelling: angels and isotopes at Yucca Mountain, Nevada. *Antipode*, **45**(2), 417–35. http://doi.org/10.1111/j.1467-8330.2012.01006.x

Hultman, M. (2017). Natures of masculinities: conceptualising industrial, eco-modern and ecological masculinities. In S. Buckingham and V. L. Masson, eds., *Understanding climate change through gender relations*, London: Routledge, pp.87–103.

Hutchings, R. (2014). Understanding of and vision for the environmental humanities. *Environmental humanities*, **4**(1), 213–20. http://doi.org/10.1215/22011919-3615007

Iovino, S. (2016). *Ecocriticism and Italy: ecology, resistance, and liberation*, London: Bloomsbury.

Iovino, S. (2019). The reverse of the sublime: dilemmas (and resources) of the Anthropocene garden. *RCC Perspectives: Transformations in Environment and Society*, **3**. http://doi.org/10.5282/rcc/8802

IPBES. (2019). *Global assessment report on biodiversity and ecosystem services of the Intergovernmental Science-Policy Platform on Biodiversity and Ecosystem Services*, Bonn: IPBES secretariat. https://ipbes.net/global-assessment-report-biodiversity-ecosystem-services

IPCC. (2019). *Climate change and land: an IPCC special report on climate change, desertification, land degradation, sustainable land management, food security, and greenhouse gas fluxes in terrestrial ecosystems*. https://www.ipcc.ch/srccl-report-download-page/

James, S. (2012). *Sex, race and class. The perspective of winning*, Oakland, CA: PM Press.

James, S. and López, N. (in press). *Our time is now. Sex, race, class and caring for people and planet*, Oakland, CA: PM Press.

Jochimsen, M. and Knobloch, U. (1997). Making the hidden visible: the importance of caring activities and their principles for any economy. *Ecological Economics*, **20**(2), 107–12. http://doi.org/10.1016/S0921-8009(95)00099-2

Kander, A., Malanima, P. and Warde, P. (2013). *Power to the people: energy in Europe over the last five centuries*, Princeton, NJ: Princeton University Press.

Kazis, R. and Grossman, R. L. (1982). *Fear at work: job blackmail, labor, and the environment*, Cleveland, OH: Pilgrim Press.

Kirchhof, A. M. and McNeill, J. R. (2019). *Nature and the iron curtain: environmental policy and social movements in communist and capitalist countries, 1945–1990*, Pittsburgh, PA: University of Pittsburgh Press.

Koch, M. (2019). Growth and degrowth in Marx's critique of political economy. In E. Chertkovskaya, A. Paulsson and S. Barca, eds., *Towards a political economy of degrowth*, London: Rowman & Littlefield International, pp. 69–82.

Kopenawa, D. and Albert, B. (2013). *The falling sky: words of a Yanomami shaman*, Cambridge, MA: The Belknap Press of Harvard University Press.

Krenak, A. (2019). *Ideias para adiar o fim do mundo*, São Paulo: Companhia das Letras.

LaDuke, W. (1999). *All our relations: native struggles for land and life*, Cambridge, MA: South End Press.

Leonardi, E. (2017). Carbon trading dogma: theoretical assumptions and practical implications of global carbon markets. *Ephemera: Theory and Politics in Organization*, **17**(1), 61–87.

Leonardi, E. (2019). Bringing class analysis back in: assessing the transformation of the value-nature nexus to strengthen the connection between degrowth and environmental justice. *Ecological Economics*, **156**, 83–90.

Linebaugh, P. (2014). *Stop, thief!: the commons, enclosures, and resistance*, Oakland, CA: PM Press.

Lorde, A. (1984). *Sister outsider: essays and speeches*, Trumansburg, NY: Crossing Press.

Lugones, M. (2010). Toward a decolonial feminism. *Hypatia*, **25**(4), 742–59. http://doi.org/10.1111/j.1527-2001.2010.01137.x

Luke, T. (1995). Sustainable development as a power/knowledge system: the problem of 'governmentality'. In F. Fischer and M. Black, eds., *Greening environmental policy: the politics of a sustainable future*, London: Paul Chapman Publishing, pp.21–32.

MacGregor, S. (2017). Gender and environment: an introduction. In S. MacGregor, ed., *Routledge handbook of gender and environment*, New York, NY: Routledge, pp. 1–24.

Mah, A. (2012). *Industrial ruination, community and place: landscapes and legacies of urban decline*, Toronto: University of Toronto Press.

Malm, A. (2016). *Fossil capital: the rise of steam-power and the roots of global warming*, London: Verso.

Malm, A. and Hornborg, A. (2014). The geology of mankind? A critique of the Anthropocene narrative. *The Anthropocene Review*, **1**(1), 62–69. http://doi.org/10.1177/2053019613516291

Martínez-Alier, J. (2002). *The environmentalism of the poor: a study of ecological conflicts and valuation*, Cheltenham, UK: Edward Elgar Publishing.

Mbembe, A. (2001). *On the postcolony*. Berkeley, CA: University of California Press.

Medina, M. (2007). *The world's scavengers. Salvaging for sustainable consumption and production*, Lanham, MD: Rowman/Altamira.

McNeill, J. R. and Engelke, P. (2014). *The great acceleration: an environmental history of the Anthropocene since 1945*, Cambridge, MA: Harvard University Press.

Mellor, M. (1996). Ecofeminism and ecosocialism: dilemmas of essentialism and materialism. In T. Benton, ed., *The greening of Marxism*, New York, NY: Guilford Publications, pp. 251–67.

Mellor, M. (2019). Care as wellth: Internalising care by democratising money. In C. Bauhardt and W. Harcourt, eds., *Feminist political ecology and the economics of care: in search of economic alternatives*, London: Routledge, pp. 116–30.

Merchant, C. (1980). *The death of nature: women, ecology, and the scientific revolution*, London: Wildwood House.

Merchant, C. (1989). *Ecological revolutions: nature, gender, and science in New England*, Chapel Hill, NC: University of North Carolina Press.

Merchant, C. (1996). *Earthcare: women and the environment*, London: Routledge.

Merchant, C. (2005). *Radical ecology: the search for a livable world*, London: Routledge.

Merchant, C. (2016). *Autonomous nature: problems of prediction and control from ancient times to the scientific revolution*, London: Routledge.

Messerschmidt, J. W. (2018). *Hegemonic masculinity: formulation, reformulation, and amplification*, Lanham, MD: Rowman & Littlefield.

Mies, M. (1986). *Patriarchy and accumulation on a world scale: women in the international division of labour*, London: Zed Books.

Mignolo, W. and Walsh, C. E. (2018). *On decoloniality: concepts, analytics, praxis*, Durham, NC: Duke University Press.

Milanez, F. (2013). War in paradise. A political ecology analysis of the scientific debate on conservation issues and human occupation of the Amazon rainforest. School of Environment and Development, University of Manchester.

Milanez, F. (2015). 'A ousadia de conviver com a floresta': uma ecologia política do extrativismo na Amazônia. PhD thesis, University of Coimbra, Coimbra. https://estudogeral.sib.uc.pt/handle/10316/29762

Milanez, F. (2019). Countering the order of progress: colonialism, extractivism and re-existence in the Brazilian Amazon. In E. Chertkovskaya, A. Paulsson and S. Barca, eds., *Towards a political economy of degrowth*, London: Rowman & Littlefield International, pp. 121–36.

Milanez, F. and Santos Pinto, M. (2017). Nego fugido y la rebelión esclava en el Antropoceno. *Ecología Política. Cuadernos de debate internacional*, **53**, 72–75.

Millán Moncayo, M. (2011). Feminismos, postcolonialidad, descolonización: ¿del centro a los márgenes? *Andamios, Revista de Investigación Social*, **8** (17), 11–36. http://doi.org/10.29092/uacm.v8i17.443

Mitman, G., Haraway, D. and Tsing, A. (2019). Reflections on the Plantationocene: a conversation with Donna Haraway and Anna Tsing. *Edge Effects*, 12 October. https://edgeeffects.net/haraway-tsing-plantationocene/

Montrie, C. (2008). *Making a living: work and environment in the United States*, Chapel Hill, NC: University of North Carolina Press.

Moore, J. W. (2000). Environmental crises and the metabolic rift in world-historical perspective. *Organization & Environment*, **13**(2), 123–57. http://doi.org/10.1177/1086026600132001

Moore, J. W. (2003). Capitalism as world-ecology: Braudel and Marx on environmental history. *Organization & Environment*, **16**(4), 514–17. http://doi.org/10.1177/1086026603259091

Moore, J. W. (2011a). Transcending the metabolic rift: a theory of crises in the capitalist world-ecology. *Journal of Peasant Studies*, **38**(1), 1–46.

Moore, J. W. (2011b). Ecology, capital, and the nature of our times: accumulation and crisis in the capitalist world-ecology. *Journal of World-Systems Research*, **17**(1), 108–47.

Moore, J. W. (2015). *Capitalism in the web of life: ecology and the accumulation of capital*, London: Verso.

Moore, J. W. (2016). Anthropocene or Capitalocene?: nature, history, and the crisis of capitalism. In J. W. Moore, ed., *Anthropocene or Capitalocene?: nature, history, and the crisis of capitalism*, Oakland, CA: PM Press, pp. 1–13.

Mortimer-Sandilands, C. and Erickson, B. (eds.). (2010). *Queer ecologies: sex, nature, politics, desire*, Bloomington, IN: Indiana University Press.

Mueller, R. (2015). Ferruccio Brugnaro: Italy's proletarian poet. *Italica*, **92**(3), 691–701.

Nelson, J. A. (1993). The study of choice or the study of provisioning? Gender and the definition of economics. In M. A. Ferber and J. A. Nelson, eds., *Beyond economic man: feminist theory and economics*, Chicago, IL: University of Chicago Press, pp. 23–36.

Nelson, J. A. and Power, M. (2018). Ecology, sustainability, and care: developments in the field. *Feminist Economics*, **24**(3), 80–8. http://doi.org/10.1080/13545701.2018.1473914

Newell, P. (2012). *Globalization and the environment: capitalism, ecology and power*, Cambridge: Polity Press.

Nightingale, A. (2006). The nature of gender: work, gender, and environment. *Environment and Planning D: Society and Space*, **24**(2), 165–85. http://doi.org/10.1068/d01k

Nixon, R. (2011). *Slow violence and the environmentalism of the poor*, Cambridge, MA: Harvard University Press.

Oppermann, S. and Iovino, S. (2016). Introduction: the environmental humanities and the challenges of the Anthropocene. In S. Oppermann and S. Iovino, eds., *Environmental humanities: voices from the Anthropocene*, London: Rowman & Littlefield International Ltd, pp. 1–22.

Oxfam International. (2019). Women defenders of the land and the environment: silenced voices. https://www.oxfam.org/en/women-defenders-land-and-environment-silenced-voices

Paredes, J. (2012). *Hilando fino: desde el feminismo comunitario.*, Querétaro: Colectivo Grietas.

Parrique, T., Barth, J. and Briens, F. et al. (2019). *Decoupling debunked: evidence and arguments against green growth as a sole strategy for sustainability*, European Environmental Bureau. https://eeb.org/library/decoupling-debunked/

Patel, R. and Moore, J. W. (2018). *A history of the world in seven cheap things: a guide to capitalism, nature, and the future of the planet*, Oakland, CA: University of California Press.

Pellow, D. N. (2000). Environmental inequality formation: toward a theory of environmental injustice. *American Behavioral Scientist*, **43**(4), 581–601. https://doi.org/10.1177/0002764200043004004

Perkins, E., Kuiper, E. and Quiroga-Martínez, R. et al. (2005). Introduction: exploring feminist ecological economics / gender, development, and sustainability from a Latin American perspective / African peasants and global gendered class struggle for the commons / ecofeminist political economy: integrating feminist economics and ecological economics / habits of thought, agency, and transformation: an institutional approach to feminist ecological economics / the network vorsorgendes wirtschaften / engendering organic farming. *Feminist Economics*, **11**(3), 107–50. http://doi.org/10.1080/13545700500301494

Perreault, T., Bridge, G. and McCarthy, J. (eds.). (2015). *The Routledge handbook of political ecology*, London: Routledge.

Piccardi, E. G. (2018). Jineoloji ed economia politica. un'introduzione alla rivoluzione delle donne in Kurdistan. In EcoPol and F. Giardini, eds., *Bodymetrics. La misura dei corpi*, Vol. 2, Rome: IAPh Italia, pp. 55–66.

Pietilä, H. (2006). The constant imperative: provisioning by cultivation and households. Paper presented at the The Ninth Biennial Conference of the International Society for Ecological Economics, 15-18 December, The India Habitat Centre, New Delhi. www.hilkkapietila.net/articles/en/economy/ ISEE_Delhi2.doc

Piketty, T. (2014). *Capital in the twenty-first century*, Cambridge, MA: Harvard University Press.

Plumwood, V. (1993). *Feminism and the mastery of nature*, London: Routledge.

Plumwood, V. (2002). *Environmental culture: the ecological crisis of reason*, London: Routledge.

Plumwood, V. (2009). Nature in the active voice. *Australian Humanities Review*, 46, 113–29. http://doi.org/10.22459/AHR.46.2009.10

Pulido, L. (1996). *Environmentalism and economic justice: two Chicano struggles in the Southwest*, Tucson, AZ: University of Arizona Press.

Pulido, L. (2018). Racism and the Anthropocene. In G. Mitman, M. Armiero and R. S. Emmett, eds., *Future remains: a cabinet of curiosities for the Anthropocene*, Chicago, IL: University of Chicago Press, pp. 116–28.

Raworth, K. (2017). *Doughnut economics: seven ways to think like a 21st-century economist*, London: Penguin Random House.

Redclift, M. (2005). Sustainable development (1987–2005): an oxymoron comes of age. *Sustainable Development*, **13**(4), 212–27. http://doi.org/10 .1002/sd.281

Roberts, J. A. and Langston, N. (2008). Toxic bodies/toxic environments: an interdisciplinary forum. *Environmental History*, **13**(4), 629–35.

Rocheleau, D. and Nirmal, P. (2015). Feminist political ecologies: grounded, networked and rooted on earth. In R. Baksh and W. Harcourt, eds., *The Oxford handbook of transnational feminist movements*, Oxford: Oxford University Press, pp. 793–814.

Rockström, J., Steffen, W. and Noone, K. et al. (2009). A safe operating space for humanity. *Nature*, **461**(7263), 472–75. http://doi.org/10.1038 /461472a

Roelvink, G. (2013). Rethinking species-being in the Anthropocene. *Rethinking Marxism*, **25**(1), 52–69. http://doi.org/10.1080/08935696.2012.654700

Salleh, A. (2009). Ecological debt: embodied debt. In A. Salleh, ed., *Eco-sufficiency and global justice: women write political ecology*, London: Pluto Press, pp. 1–41.

Salleh, A. (2010). From metabolic rift to 'metabolic value': reflections on environmental sociology and the alternative globalization movement. *Organization & Environment*, **23**(2), 205–19. http://doi.org/10.1177 /1086026610372134

Salleh, A. (2016). The Anthropocene: thinking in 'deep geological time' or deep libidinal time? *International Critical Thought*, **6**(3), 422–33. http://doi .org/10.1080/21598282.2016.1197784

Salleh, A. (2017 [1997]). *Ecofeminism as politics: nature, Marx and the postmodern*, 2nd edition, London: Zed Books.

Sandilands, C. (2016). Queer ecology. In J. Adamson, W. A. Gleason and D. N. Pellow, eds., *Keywords for environmental studies*, New York, NY: New York University Press, pp. 169–71.

Sapp Moore, S., Allewaert, M., Gómez, P. F. and Mitman, G. (2019). Plantation legacies. *Edge Effects*, 22 January. http://edgeeffects.net/plantation-legacies-plantationocene/

Schmelzer, M. (2016). *The hegemony of growth: the OECD and the making of the economic growth paradigm*, Cambridge: Cambridge University Press.

Schnaiberg, A. (1980). *The environment, from surplus to scarcity*, Oxford: Oxford University Press.

Schutz, E. A. (2011). *Inequality and power: the economics of class*, London: Routledge.

Seger, M. (2015). *Landscapes in between: environmental change in modern Italian literature and film*, Toronto: University of Toronto Press.

Sellers, C. and Melling, J. (2012). Introduction. From dangerous trades to trade in dangers: toward an industrial hazard history of the present. In C. Sellers and J. Melling, eds., *Dangerous trade: histories of industrial hazard across a globalizing world*, Philadelphia, PA: Temple University Press, pp. 1–14.

Sousa Santos, B. (2014). *Epistemologies of the south: justice against epistemicide*, London: Routledge.

Spaargaren, G. and Mol, A. P. J. (1992). Sociology, environment, and modernity: ecological modernization as a theory of social change. *Society & Natural Resources*, **5**(4), 323–44. http://doi.org/10.1080/08941929209380797

Steffen, W., Richardson, K. and Rockstrom, J. et al. (2015). Planetary boundaries: guiding human development on a changing planet. *Science*, **347**(6223), 1259855. http://doi.org/10.1126/science.1259855

Stengers, I. (2015). *In catastrophic times: resisting the coming barbarism*, Lüneburg:Open Humanities Press.

Svampa, M. (2019). *Neo-extractivism in Latin America: socio-environmental conflicts, the territorial turn, and new political narratives*, Cambridge: Cambridge University Press.

Swyngedouw, E. and Ernstson, H. (2018). Interrupting the Anthropo-obscene: immuno-biopolitics and depoliticizing ontologies in the Anthropocene. *Theory, Culture & Society*, **35**(6), 3–30. http://doi.org/10.1177/0263276418757314

Taylor, D. E. (2016). *The rise of the American conservation movement: power, privilege, and environmental protection*, Durham, NC: Duke University Press.

Tola, M. (2018). Between Pachamama and Mother Earth: gender, political ontology and the rights of nature in contemporary Bolivia. *Feminist Review*, **118**(1), 25–40. http://doi.org/10.1057/s41305-018-0100-4

Tola, M. (2019). The archive and the lake. *Environmental humanities*, **11**(1), 194–215. http://doi.org/10.1215/22011919-7349499

Tsing, A. (2012). Unruly edges: mushrooms as companion species: for Donna Haraway. *Environmental humanities*, **1**(1), 141–54. http://doi.org/10.1215/22011919-3610012

Turco, A. (2018). *La città a sei zampe. Cronaca industriale, ambientale e operaia di uno tra i maggiori petrolchimici d'Europa*, Catania: Villaggio Maori.

Turner, T. E. and Brownhill, L. S. (2004). Why women are at war with Chevron: Nigerian subsistence struggles against the international oil industry. *Journal of Asian and African Studies*, **39**(1–2), 63–93. http://doi.org/10.1177/0021909604048251

van Horssen, J. (2016). *A town called asbestos: environmental contamination, health, and resilience in a resource community*, Vancouver: UBC Press.

Viveiros de Castro, E. (2015). 'Alguma coisa vai ter que acontecer'. In S. Cohn, ed., *Ailton Krenak*, Rio de Janeiro: Azougue, pp.8–19.

Walsh, C. (2015). Life, nature and gender otherwise: feminist reflections and provocations from the Andes. In W. Harcourt and I. L. Nelson, eds., *Practising feminist political ecologies: moving beyond the 'green economy'*, London: Zed Books, pp. 101–30.

Waring, M. (1999). *Counting for nothing: what men value and what women are worth*, 2nd edition, Toronto: University of Toronto Press.

Warlenius, R., Pierce, G., Ramasar, V., Quistorp, E., Martínez-Alier, J., Rijnhout, L. and Yanez, I. (2015). Ecological debt. History, meaning and relevance for environmental justice. *EJOLT*, 18. www.ejolt.org/2015/01/concept-ecological-debt-value-environmental-justice/

White, D., Rudy, A. and Gareau, B. (2016). *Environments, natures and social theory: towards a critical hybridity*, London: Palgrave Macmillan.

Whyte, K. P. (2017). Our ancestors' dystopia now: Indigenous conservation and the Anthropocene. In U. K. Heise, J. Christensen and M. Niemann, eds., *The Routledge companion to the environmental humanities*, London: Routledge.

Wrigley, E. A. (1988). *Continuity, chance and change: the character of the industrial revolution in England*, Cambridge: Cambridge University Press.

Ziglioli, B. (2016). *Sembrava nevicasse: La Eternit di Casale Monferrato e la Fibronit di Broni: due comunità di fronte all'amianto*, Milan: Franco Angeli.

Acknowledgements

This work comes out of inspirations I received from the academic and political networks within which I have been embedded for the past ten years. These are: first and foremost, the European network of Political Ecology (ENTiTLE), now a scholarly/activist collective, and its *Undisciplined environments* blog; the Ecosoc (Ecology and Society) Lab at the Centre for Social Studies in Coimbra (Portugal); the international communities of Historical Materialism, Degrowth, Environmental Labor Studies and the WEGO (Feminist Political Ecology) network; the Italian POE (Politics Ontology Ecology) and EPP (*Ecologie Politiche del Presente*) networks, as well as various Italian students' collectives with which I have interacted in the past two years; environmental justice activists and scientists that I have met in Manfredonia, Taranto, Naples and Campania; and many more.

I am immensely grateful to Felipe Milanez for sharing with me his knowledge of Zé Claudio's and Maria's lives, and much more; and for inviting me to the Third Latin American Political Ecology conference, which took place in Salvador de Bahia in March 2019. I am indebted to the Indigenous, Quilombo and Amazonian speakers at that conference (and especially to Edel Moraes, Ângela Mendes, Sonja Guajajara, Alessandra Munduruku, Elionice Sacramento and Bernadete Ferreira Santos) who shared their visions and practices of re/existence against the environmental violence of the Anthropocene. I am aware that this book does not do justice to the relevance and sophistication of their narratives, but I hope it will contribute in some way to their struggles to decolonize environmental thought and politics. I am also very grateful to my friends (colleagues and students) from the Centre for Social Studies in Coimbra for their help in the thought process that led to this Element – and especially to Francisco Venes, Gaia Giuliani, Emanuele Leonardi, Gea Piccardi and Roberto Sciarelli, for their comments on the first draft.

Overall, this work is deeply indebted to that of Carolyn Merchant and Ariel Salleh, two politically engaged scholars with whom I have had the fortune of crossing paths at various moments of my life, who have greatly inspired my vision of feminist ecosocialism. Over the past few months, the encounter with life-long activist Selma James has opened my mind through her fascinating intellectual clarity and determination. I am deeply honoured by the thought that she and her companion Nina López think of me as a kindred soul.

Last but not least, I wish to thank Serenella Iovino, Timo Maran and Louise Wrestling for including me in the great adventure of this Element series, and for their exceptional editorial support; to Serenella I send my endless gratitude for enthusiastically believing in this project, and for the invaluable intellectual and emotional gifts I have received from her over the years.

This publication results from financial support from the Portuguese Foundation for Science and Technology through its pluriannual funding for R&D units (UIDP/50012/2020).

Cambridge Elements ≡

Environmental Humanities

Louise Westling
University of Oregon

Timo Maran
University of Tartu

Serenella Iovino
University of North Carolina at Chapel Hill

About the Series

The environmental humanities is a new transdisciplinary complex of approaches to the embeddedness of human life and culture in all the dynamics that characterize the life of the planet. These approaches reexamine our species' history in light of the intensifying awareness of drastic climate change and ongoing mass extinction. To engage this reality, Cambridge Elements in Environmental Humanities builds on the idea of a more hybrid and participatory mode of research and debate, connecting critical and creative fields.

Cambridge Elements ☰

Environmental Humanities

Elements in the Series

Printed in the United States
By Bookmasters